JOYS,
SORROWS,
AND
SHADOWS

*by one
who experienced
the joys, sorrows, and shadows*

DEDICATED
to my husband,
Omer King.
Without his inspiration
and encouragement,
I would not have consented
to publish this book.

The photograph on the front cover
was taken by Richard Reinhold,
Intelligencer Journal Photographer.
The first buggy in the
funeral procession is the hearse.

The only names changed in this book
were Danny Biller, Tom Anderson,
Hans and Leona Biller (Danny's parents),
and the jury foreman.

Designed and Printed by
Olde Springfield Shoppe
10 West Main Street, P. O. Box 171
Elverson, PA 19520-0171

Contents

AN AUNT

I hold no quarrel with the world
O'er which our lives are spanned.
The more I see its ways unfurled
I find things wisely planned,
Though some believe that circumstances
Shape all our joys, I can't;
I'm certain it was more than chance
That gave our babes an Aunt.

When first this race of ours began
And little ones were few,
Think you that in the mind of man
The Aunt idea grew?
I fancy that the Lord did
Who guards the tenderest plant.
Looked down and said, "For boundless love,
That baby needs an Aunt."

They cannot all have children there
For that would never do.
There must be some with time to spare
To mind the babies, too.
There must be some to give them joys—
A mother simply can't,
And so the little girls and boys,
Shall also have an Aunt."

Now Aunts are everywhere about
Their gifts of love to bring
To whisper when the youngsters shout,
"Oh, let them have their fling."
And next unto a Mother's love
The tenderest love extant
Is that which marks the conduct of
A good old-fashioned Aunt.

—— Introduction ——

This is an unusual but true account of a deep tragedy which took place in our family on the evening of November 27, 1982.

Being a writer, I felt the need to express my feelings on paper in order to dispose my thoughts and get them out of my system for they were like poison inside me. Writing down my feelings has done the work of a psychiatrist for me....

I wrote this journal two years after the tragedy took place with no intentions of anyone else reading it. Soon after the tragedy, people asked us if we had ever thought of writing a book about this happening. No, we thought we could never do that for we wanted to forget that it ever happened. As the years rolled on, our thinking became more realistic and we realized that we cannot avoid the fact that it **did** happen, and we owe it to the next generation to give them an accurate account of the happening instead of a distorted one. However, it should not be read by children and probably not by young teenagers either.

After I had written this journal in 1984, I packed it away where it stayed until recently when my sister asked to read it. She read it—and when others heard about it, she passed it on to them. It was my only copy and I finally asked to have it back. Since there were still others who wanted to read it, someone suggested that I get it printed. I was very hesitant for I had not written this for fame or for pity. Rather, it is my wish that it could be of help to someone in similar circumstances or any kind of sorrow.

Christians are taught to bear each other's burdens, but how can that be done if no one shares?

Other family members would each have their own version of the tragedy if they were to relate it. This is only mine.

A lot of this writing was done in Aunt Mary's kitchen on winter days. I would write until 3:30 p.m. and then get up and leave for that was the time that Aunt Naomi usually came home from work. But she wasn't coming home to us anymore—for she was the victim of this tragedy. While I was so deep in writing, I could almost see Naomi walking in the door at 3:30. I would feel as if I was having illusions and was filled with a deep sadness.

Finally, after all these years the hurt is not quite as deep, but it is still there. We cannot "live" on memories—so we will remember our loved ones as the gentlest of flowers, now blooming in heaven. We want to continue in life, looking upward and onward, and not faint by the way.

Emma King

v

Chapter 1

We were an ordinary Amish family of nine children living on a farm one mile north of New Holland in Lancaster County, Pennsylvania.

There were two houses practically against each other on the farm. We lived in one house and Grandma Huyard lived in the other house with her two single daughters—my aunts—until Grandma died in 1967. I was eleven years old then and it was my first encounter with death in our direct family.

My twin sister and I were Grandma's "pets," and we practically grew up in her house. Mother told us that we crawled over to Grandma's before we could walk. It took us a long time to get over Grandma's death.

Our two aunts—Mary and Naomi—always meant a great deal to all of us, too. Mary had been a schoolteacher for thirty-two terms at the time of this writing and was still teaching.

Her sister, Naomi, worked for her brothers and sisters in her younger years. She worked for our family for seven years. The last fifteen years of her life, she worked in the laundry of a nursing home until she met an untimely death on November 27, 1982, at the age of fifty.

In 1982, there were five of us children living at home and we were all in our twenties except for Levi who was thirty-four, the oldest and mentally retarded. My older sister, Rebecca, my two brothers, Stevie and Amos, and I were at home yet.

My older sisters, Susie and Sara, were both married for a number of years and lived away from home. My twin sister, Esther, lived near Ephrata and was married for five years. A brother, Mose, was single and lived by himself in New Holland.

Aunt Mary and Aunt Naomi always felt like a combined Grandma/ Mother/Sister to us. Most of my evenings as far back as I can remember were spent at the Aunts' house. On warm summer evenings, we would sit on the open porch and read or chat. Winter evenings would find us sitting beside the stove to write, sew, and chat while Aunt Mary would do her school work.

They subscribed to the daily evening paper which would lure the boys over to their house. It was common to see two of the boys sprawled full length on the floor as they read the news. Naomi always loved to tease Levi. Sometimes when he was in a bad mood, he would punch or pinch her. Then she'd tell him to rub it for her and he would! If the aunts needed any repairs done, it would be the boys who would respond.

Many a winter evening or Sunday, we would ask Naomi to relate details of our babyhood. We would never have learned many of these details, if it would not have been for her willingness to share.

Esther and I always had this thing going about tea parties with Naomi in the evenings. Mary was bored with us at times. During the summer, we would dry lots of tea for our winter evenings. Sometimes when Mary had an extra pile of school work that she wanted to do, she would almost get cross at us when we'd be chatting on and on because it distracted her. But it was usually funny to us because after we would relate something funny, Mary would also join in the laughing when we thought she didn't even hear our conversation. This became quite a game for us.

Then there were those evenings when I wanted to write letters and Naomi was in the mood to chat! I couldn't very well do both at the same time, so I'd end up ignoring her chatter and responding with an occasional "yes" or "uh-huh." Finally, she would become impatient and say, "If you just want to write, you'd better go home!" Most times I could not resist that and would end up quitting my writing to chat with her.

Naomi just loved to have her hair combed, so many an evening was spent taking her hair down and brushing and rebrushing it. Then sometimes we would style her hair in different ways which would amuse her. When we didn't show up an evening or two, Naomi would notice it and would ask when we're coming again!

Actually, growing up with two single aunts and seeing their lifestyle appealed to us girls so much that it instilled in our minds that it would be a very nice way to live. When we discussed this with Naomi, she would tell us that we must not remain single just because they did. She said that we would become lonely when we got older.

Then we would respond, "She's not lonely."

But Aunt Naomi would tell us that she was not old yet herself, and she wondered who would take care of her when she got old. I remember of frequently reassuring her that she need never worry about that because any of us children would gladly care for her. But that never seemed to satisfy her.

How little did we know what the future would hold for her, and it's good that we did not know. It certainly proves how small we humans actually are. Now she has already gone to Eternity.

As happens in any family life, we sometimes had our disagreements and at times could have been kinder to each other. But, in general, we enjoyed each other very much and our life pattern flowed smoothly. We loved and understood each other.

Since Aunt Naomi is the main character throughout this book,

I will relate some of her character and personality. She was the second to the youngest of eight children, and in some ways it felt like everyone "used" her. When her brothers and sisters (and others in the community) needed help, they came to her. She was always there to help.

Aunt Naomi was only four feet and ten inches tall and never weighed over one hundred pounds. She was very bashful around men and self-conscious in groups. There were many times when she would arrive home from a wedding or large group gathering or even church and was very tense just because she was in the presence of others. If she entertained company in her home, she was the same way. Afterwards, she would beg me to treat her feet and neck to relax her. Many, many times I did this for her.

She never liked to have attention drawn to herself, but she appreciated when individuals noticed her and talked with her because she felt inferior to others. She was not what anyone would call a popular person and was overly-conscientious with her dealings with people and also her job at the Home.

She was required to work every fourth Sunday at the nursing home and despised it. But, she never punched in any time for Sundays because she never wanted to be paid for working on Sundays. I believe that she received a blessing for this because someone does need to care for elderly people on Sundays, too.

She greatly appreciated if one of her nieces, brothers, or sisters wanted to help her on a Sunday and then bring her back home. Many times Esther and I would go with her. Sometimes we would go with her on a Saturday evening and stay at the Home overnight. That way she didn't have to work so long on Sunday. Naomi had a child-like spirit and loved to play games with us. She loved small parties, especially with a bunch of girls. She enjoyed fun. She practically lived for her nieces and nephews which made her a special pet to all of them. The Aunts' home was a hang-out for the nieces and nephews and some even called it "the Aunt Hill."

She also lived for others in addition to her family. She wrote many letters and often visited the sick. Attending church was very important to her and she kept a complete record of where the services were held and who had the sermon.

If there was a funeral or any type of trouble in the neighborhood, she was usually the person to be called upon. There was many a Sunday when we girls would have no special plans and she would coax us to stay for dinner. Occasionally, Aunt Mary was not home overnight, and Aunt Naomi would ask us to stay overnight so she wouldn't be alone.

Three weeks before she died on a Saturday night when she was alone, I went over to visit. She asked if I had brought my nightie along. I told her that I didn't, but I would get it. So I stayed with her that night.

In her way, she was outspoken and, consequently, misunderstood at times. But it always hurt her when she knew that she had wronged or hurt someone. She was very generous, but also very economical. She wore a lot of patched clothing at times when there was no need for it. We often teased her about her patches, but she would laugh and tell us that she was raised not to be wasteful.

It was quite an honor to her when we would introduce our young friends to her or tell about our weekend activities with the young folks. At that time, we did not think about how much she appreciated our sharing because it was the customary thing to do in our daily schedule. Looking back now, I know she appreciated it very much.

Aunt Naomi had a cataract operation on her eye in 1969 which left her with poor eyesight for a while until she purchased contact lenses. But her eyes did not accept the contacts, so she ended up wearing heavy cataract glass lenses in a frame. We read many books to her that winter, and also played many a game with her.

She was very faithful with her work at the nursing home and seldom took a day off unless it was her usual weekly day off on Tuesday. On that free day, she would usually help one of her brothers or sisters. If not that, then she would often help Mom quilt.

Her main work at home was cooking and the laundry work. I can still hear her singing above the sound of the washing machine motor, "Wash Me and I Shall Be Whiter Than Snow." But the song that she sang the most was, "Just over the stars; Just over the beautiful stars; By the bloodwashed throne, we'll sing sweet home; In a land just over the stars."

Another main point in her home life was the way we would always depend on her to fetch the daily mail. Her usual time to come home from work was 3:30 p.m., and she would always bring the mail along. We could depend on seeing her small figure hurrying in the lane at that time. She would often stop at our house and Mom would make her a cup of coffee. If Mom was quilting, Naomi would sit down and help awhile until it was time for her to leave and make her supper. Then I would time it perfectly so that I would arrive at their house in the evening just after they were finished eating, so that I could eat leftovers. They almost expected my arrival after doing this for some time.

Even now, two years after Naomi's death, I catch myself glancing out the lane involuntarily expecting to see Naomi carrying the mail in to us. Then suddenly the realization of her death hits me!

Naomi was the type of person who would trust almost everyone! In the summer of 1980, a fourteen-year-old girl, Evelyn Fisher, of New Holland was missing for three months and was finally found dead in the nearby woods tied up and cruelly murdered. This event shook our entire neighborhood. Many people, including my brothers, helped to search for her. I was badly shaken by this and it placed a wariness and fear in me I had not previously experienced.

At times in the evenings when we discussed this with the aunts, it would chill me. I would feel extremely scared to run home those few yards in the dark. More than once, Naomi stood at her door, at my request, until she saw that I was home. This did amuse her. It seemed as though she was naive to the evil that surrounds us. If she ever experienced any fear of people, we never sensed it.

We lived in a nice neighborhood with about fifteen houses across the street (and across the field) from our farm. We knew most of our neighbors—all very nice—though we did not visit that much. We visited with the Tresslers the most.

The Hans Biller family lived directly across the field from our house. They were living there for about fifteen years and were Mennonites, although, in some ways seemed different. I don't mean to say this to degrade them—I am only being frank in my description. It seemed as if their other neighbors also looked upon them as different. We always tried to be neighborly, and we could tell that they appreciated it.

Hans worked at night, so Leona would sometimes bring her two little adopted boys—Raymond and Danny—to visit with us in the evening. These boys were adopted as babies. Leona would sit and sit and didn't realize that we were ready for bed. Dad would finally go to bed and then complain about this to Mom. But Mom always took pity on Leona and said that she needed someone to talk with her.

Raymond and Danny would be shut in their basement every forenoon because their Dad needed to sleep. Idle hands and minds are the devil's workshop, and it seemed ironic that later on in his life, the basement was the place that Danny picked to accomplish his devilment.

Sometimes in the summertime, the Biller boys would come out to the farm to play. We were usually working, but we'd let them play. As they got older we didn't like it so well, for they grew bolder. One time Mom scolded Danny after she saw him sneaking in the bedroom door. Another time when I was out helping to do chores in the evening, I went back to the haymow and there I caught Danny holding a lighted match to a bale of hay. I quickly stopped him and went in the house to Mom with him and told her about it. She gave him a severe scolding, but with those boys, one was never sure if your words sank in or not, for they wore blank

5

expressions and hardly ever smiled. They seemed to be born losers. Danny may have been twelve at the time of this episode.

After that I can't remember that they ever came to play anymore. They had a rough time at school and were expelled for misbehavior and had to change schools. It also created problems in their home.

One evening the boys came running into our house after dark, and they were crying. They might have been ten or eleven then and we did pity them. They said their mother was running away, so Dad went along out with them and learned that Leona said she was going to walk off. She started walking up the road and this scared the boys. Of course, she came back again. In short, I think most people who knew them felt they were too old to adopt babies, while the Billers, themselves, thought they were doing a good deed.

After the boys were over the age of fourteen, we hardly saw them anymore, but we still kept track of them somewhat. They were both in State Correctional Centers at a young age for stealing, etc. Several times they were caught stealing from some of the neighbors.

One night at the Tresslers, when their daughter was at home alone, she was awakened to the sound of breaking glass. She got up, snapped on the lights, and heard someone fleeing. When she got downstairs, no one was around, but the glass door was broken. The next day a knife was found outside the house with Danny's initials on it. The Tresslers gave it to the police, but the police couldn't do anything about it because Danny wasn't caught in the act.

We knew that Danny carried a knife and we knew that he had sexual hangups, for once he was caught, along with another guy, for a robbery in town and they had rooted through underwear drawers. In spite of all this, we trusted Danny and Raymond because we figured they respected us and we were not afraid of them at all.

Danny joined the Army at one point but then left without official leave and was later jailed for that. We hardly knew they existed anymore those last years. Later we learned that every time the neighbors knew that one of the Biller boys was home again, even just for a weekend, they would call each other as a warning. If their parents weren't home when they got there and the house was locked, they would break in the basement window. This is how Danny got in the last time he was home in October 1982. His own mother told us she was afraid of him, which is probably why he was forbidden to come home anymore; yet, when he did come home, they left him stay. It is now our theory that Danny's parents were afraid for themselves if they would deny him this.

We were hardly back and forth with the Billers at all anymore, except to go out to the freezer, which we had in their garage. This arrangement

6

came about soon after the Billers moved to our neighborhood. Mom had mentioned to Leona that there had been a fire at the place where our lockers had been and we lost all our frozen goods. Since we have no electricity in our home, Leona offered that we could use a freezer in their garage, so the arrangement was made that we would take care of their trash in exchange for the use of their electricity. Levi always took care of the trash, although I don't think we kept our end of this deal as well as we should have. But, is that relevant to what happened, or any excuse for the events that took place later?

The last time that I had seen Danny was a week before this happening, in November 1982. I was driving home from town with a horse-and-buggy and it was already dark. Suddenly, to my right, I saw a figure walking on the bank alongside of the road. At first glance, I thought it was a girl, for the person had long blond hair which hung to his shoulders and swayed back and forth as he walked. But I soon saw that it was Danny, with his quick movements. I waved to him and he waved back. I thought of offering him a ride, but something deep inside of me told me I should be afraid of him. I thought about him as I drove home and wondered what he was doing with his life. None of us realized that he was home for several weeks that fall. Later, Stevie said that if he would have known that Danny was around, he would have warned us to be careful.

In the spring of 1981, my twin sister and her husband, David, were blessed with twin boys, which were their first children. Naturally, everyone was excited about this. Naomi was as excited as we were and could hardly wait to see them. But she kept saying she was afraid they'd be spoiled! Yet she was one of the worst to show them off. I must admit this rather irratated me. She even persisted until David and Esther arranged a day to take the twins up to the nursing home to show them to the old people. They were four months old then and very active. Naomi took a great interest in them. I think they brought back memories of us to Naomi. They were two cute, blond, blue-eyed look-alikes. David and Esther took them to the Home only to please Naomi and I guess it was worth the effort, for it made those people very happy!

Naomi loved those old people. One of our non-Amish friends who visited Naomi at the Home one day said to us, "It seems as if those old people reached out to her as if she was an angel."

In the fall of 1981, on November 19, a sudden, sad death struck our family. At the age of seven months, one of the baby twins died in his sleep. They had been perfectly healthy babies. The doctor pronounced it crib death, but we will never know what actually took place, as we still feel at times that he smothered in his blankets. However, we never doubted the will of God in this.

7

I happened to be at David's when the baby died and it was very, very sad. Esther and I called home early in the morning to tell them. Naomi had not left for work yet and she did not go to work that day. She quickly arranged for someone else to take her place that day. That was how she was—always putting others before herself. She went along to David's that morning, and I can still see her face as she walked in the door, tears streaming down her face. She asked, "Why did he have to be born, only to die so soon?" We had no answer for her. But we did come to the realization that it is better to have "loved and lost," than not to have loved at all.

We discussed it between us, that we wonder if this experience was given to us to prepare us for greater things which are yet to come. How little we realized that exactly a year later our thoughts would be quite real.

Almost a year later, in October 1982, I asked Naomi if she'd like to go along to David's with me. I was used to driving by myself with the horse and buggy, but for some reason I wanted company that day. She readily agreed! As we were driving on Route 322, about four miles from David's, one of the shaft clips broke off. I gave Naomi the lines, jumped out, and guided the horse off the road. While doing this, the other clip broke off! The horse used good common sense and just stood there while I held him and Naomi unhitched him. Naomi was scared. There stood the carriage with no shafts. Some men soon stopped and pushed the carriage on the lawn of the Agway Store. We led the horse up the road to the nearest barn where a passerby picked us up and took us the rest of the way to David's.

It was the only time that I asked anyone to go with me. And it was Stevie's team, the team I usually took to go up there. Why did I ask her to go along that day? I felt that she saved me from what could have been a bad accident, especially since the horse was not a tame horse. How could I have managed alone? I told Naomi so. It was a day to go down "memory's lane." She hugged Esther that day, like she usually did. We often hugged her because she liked this. All those things are only memories now....

On the evening of November 19, Naomi suggested that we all go up to David's, since it was a year that twin Johnny died, so that is what we did. It was again a symbol of how she cared about others.

The following week, unknown to us, was to be her last week on earth. That week I felt unusually depressed and didn't know why. At a wedding that I attended on Thanksgiving Day, I had a long talk with a good friend of mine. We talked quite a bit about life and death, and I was not in a gay mood. I guess maybe if nothing would have happened, it would have passed by and I wouldn't have given those feelings much thought afterwards. After the tragedy happened, that same friend said that all she could think of after she heard the news was the way I had talked to her at the wedding.

On Tuesday, November 23, we all attended a church wedding. It was a cold, clear week. On Wednesday evening, just before dark, I was raking leaves between the two houses. Naomi opened her window and chatted with me and asked me if I was coming over for tea tonight. I said I would. She always liked to discuss the happenings, etc., after a wedding. That evening we got unexpected company so I did not go over to the aunts'.

Thursday, November 25, was Thanksgiving Day and we were all again invited to a church wedding at Emanuel Lapp's. Most of the church women have remarked afterward how they have such a clear picture of Naomi that day, for at the supper table she was extra lively and she was sort of everyone's target that evening. When my parents were ready to go home that evening, Naomi said to Mom that she wants to look at the bridal corner and the tables, so she went back in and looked over all the tables before she left for home. To our knowledge, this was something she never did before. Some of the church women had also noticed this and remarked about it later.

On Friday, November 26, after Naomi came home from work and came over with the mail, Mom made a cup of coffee for her. I already had my clothes on to go outdoors to rake leaves, but when Naomi came in, I sat in the big stuffed chair and Naomi sat on the arm of the chair. Then she told me I had let her down on Wednesday evening because I didn't come over for tea, and she begged me to come over that evening. I didn't promise anything because I was tired from going to weddings that week. She told us that another set of twins was born, which she noticed in the paper, and we tried to figure out who it was. We finally figured it out and the rest of our conversation was small talk. I went out to rake leaves before she left. The last living picture I have of her was her sitting on the arm of my chair.

I didn't go over that evening for I wanted to retire early for a change. I figured there would be many other evenings. Little did I know that our whole life and thought pattern would change so drastically until the following day was over. Of course, I would have gone over to chat with Naomi that evening if I would have known it was her last night on earth—but what would I have said? If any of us would know beforehand the hour of our loved one's departure, what would we do or say?

We had no way of knowing....

9

———— Chapter 2 ————

On Saturday, November 27, 1982, our day started out in our usual Saturday schedule, except that Esther came up in the morning and went along to work at People's Restaurant with Rebecca and me. In the afternoon she was at home with us. Around 3:30-4:00, she decided to head for home. She talked of stopping at the freezer to pick up her meat which she had stored there for several weeks, but then it got too late. Afterward we felt she was not supposed to stop there! That very day Mom remarked to us that she can't understand why our meat supply is so low already. She said she wonders if the Biller boys would steal meat. Then she said, "If they're that hungry, they may have the meat."

Naomi was at work that day, the same as usual. I did not see her at all, but, if the day would have proceeded as normal, I would have been at their house that evening. Mother said she saw her through the windows around 4:00 doing her ironing. Later, when we asked Mary what Naomi was doing when she came home from work, she said Naomi seemed to be in a hurry. She helped Mary put comforters on the beds and then she was ironing for a short while. Then she went to the garden and brought in some heads of cauliflower and laid them on the table saying to Mary, "What will we do with all this cauliflower?"

Mary then went outdoors to rake leaves. A few minutes later, Naomi came out with her coat and scarf on, a basket in her hand, and walked past Mary. She gave Mary a bright look while walking past, but no words were exchanged and she hurried out the lane. Mary knew, without asking, that Naomi was heading out to the freezer with the cauliflower to Billers' garage which was in full view of where Mary was raking.

Mary kept on raking until after dark, but she didn't notice the darkness because it was a bright, full-moon night. It is unusual that there are two full moons in one month, but that night it was the second full moon for that month. Different people mentioned it since the happening that often something out of the ordinary occurs when there are two full moons in one month.

The police told us later that mental patients, or people with wicked or distorted minds, definitely are influenced by the full moon. They said when they are on duty on full-moon nights, they just know they will be called out somewhere.

After Mary was in the house a short while, she wondered what was taking Naomi so long. Soon after our supper, at approximately 5:45 p.m., she came over to our house and wondered if Naomi was with us or if we had seen her. She told us she went out to the freezer and wasn't back yet, but she thought maybe Naomi might have walked to her brother Levi's, since she had talked of going there to help mix pie crusts for their wedding. So Mary wasn't worried and neither were we. After Mary left, we mentioned that it was strange that Naomi would have walked to Levi's when it was almost dark and Mary said she did not take a flashlight along. Also, it was very unlike her to go without telling someone where she was going. But we thought she could have gotten a sudden notion to walk to Levi's and they would bring her home. We pushed it back in our minds, although we were uneasy.

After Mary left our home, she waited a short while, then decided to go out to the freezer to check, although she didn't tell us she was going. As she walked into the breezeway leading to the garage, she saw a figure with its back turned, reaching up at the clothesline at the other end of the breezeway. Since it was dark, she didn't see who it was, but when hearing the door open, the figure turned, looked at her, and that quickly disappeared through the kitchen door. Mary opened the side door leading into the garage, walked over to the freezer, and looked in. She saw Naomi's basket lying on its side in the freezer so she turned around and left.

Mary went home and ate supper. After she had eaten, she came over to us again and told us that Naomi wasn't back yet. It must have been around 7:00 p.m. then. She told us what she saw out in the freezer and said she now feels sure Naomi must have gone to Levi's...(after putting her basket in the freezer), and said she isn't worried. We didn't say much because we didn't want her to see how worried we were. I thought to myself, "If Mary isn't worried, why is her face so flushed?"

As soon as she was out the door, we all sort of jumped up. We felt sure something was wrong! My first thoughts were—"maybe she was kidnapped on the road, but why was her basket in the freezer in the Biller garage?" None of us liked the idea of that basket lying in the freezer.

We wrote a note for Levi to take to Uncle Levi's, Ike's, and Elam's, asking if she's there or had been there. We gave Levi strict orders to return immediately with the note.

I got a book and tried to occupy myself by reading. Levi was hardly gone more than fifteen minutes until he returned with the note which they had written. "No, she was not here." Then we took action! We told Mary about it. We then decided that maybe she had gone through the fields to one of those places and had fallen or had a heart attack.

In my mind I couldn't picture that. A lot of scenes can flash through one's mind in an instant at such a time. Dad lighted a lantern and said he'd go out to the Biller home. Rebecca and Amos got flashlights and went out to John Marsh's who lived directly at the end of our lane. Rebecca said she would get John to take her to Levi's, Ike's, and Elam's again, and if she's not there, they'll start looking through the fields. Amos said he would check at the phone shanty across the fields. Stevie was not at home. He had left for Clinton County the day before and wanted to be out the following week for several days for deer hunting. How we wished he was home!

I got my coat and book and told Mom I was going over to Mary. I was already beginning to feel eerie. When Dad went out the door with his lantern, I slipped out with him and walked with him to Mary's door. Mary did not say much and neither did I. I tried to read, but I could not concentrate. Finally, I could not bear the silence any longer so I asked Mary, "Where do you think she is?" She said she still thinks she might have gone to one of her brothers. I shook my head in despair behind her back. Then there was silence again.

Mary started cleaning windows at the kitchen sink. She was really scrubbing them and I wondered to myself where she got the strength; I felt completely drained. I was thinking, "What's the use of cleaning windows if something happened to Naomi?" I tried to pray, but I wondered what I should pray for. Should I pray for Naomi's safety if she was already in trouble or dead? I felt so very helpless; I guess we all did. The lump in my throat kept getting bigger. Finally, the tears started to flow. Then I said to Mary, "Let's face it—if Naomi could come back by herself, she certainly would be here by now." She said, "Do you think so?" Yes, I did think so and I believe Mary thought so too by then.

I turned my back and let the tears flow. I remember looking at the clock and thinking, "Now it's 8:45 and Naomi isn't here yet." Then Mom came over and we exchanged a few words, but what was there to say? She soon went home again.

Shortly after that, Amos and Rebecca came in and said they had gone over the main trails in the fields with John Marsh's car and saw no signs of her and now they will call the police. They first called Mose to see what he would suggest, but his answering service said he was at the mountains deer hunting.

Rebecca got John Marsh to dial the number to call the police because her hands were shaking too much to do it herself. They first called Don Troupe, a policeman who lived across the field from us, and he called the Ephrata State Police Barracks. People have asked us since then how it came about that we got police help so quickly. Normally, in the case of a missing adult, the police do not respond within the first twenty-four hours because how do they know the person did not just run away. We had not known this. In this case, the police did not hesitate because our

13

neighbor Don Troupe knew Naomi personally and he knew something definitely had to be wrong.

Trooper James Nettles met Rebecca at the Marsh home and together they came to our door where Mary met them. To see an officer stand at your door, for the reason he came, is a feeling that cannot be described. One part of your mind is thinking, "This can't be real!" The other part felt so relieved to see an officer because it gave you a feeling that "finally" you have help to depend on. Maybe **he** can do something!

He asked for Naomi's description, age, and size, then said they will check all the logical places first and search all our buildings. If she was not here, they would call the fire company. Mary told him Naomi could not be in any of our buildings for she saw her walking out the lane. Nettles gave her a strange look and said in a quiet voice, "We've seen stranger things than that."

I asked him if he knew anything about Danny Biller and reminded him that Naomi was headed for the Biller home. He answered, "I know him personally." By that time, in the back of my mind, I had a feeling Danny might know something of her whereabouts, for we knew by then that Danny was home.

Rebecca had first called over to the Biller home from the Marshes to see what she could learn and Danny answered the phone. She felt afraid to go over to the home. While she was calling, Dad was at the door of the Biller home and Hans Biller and Danny came to the door.

I wondered to myself why the police didn't just go and question Danny—but little did we realize the red tape that is involved in such a case, and how extremely careful the police have to be before even just suspecting anyone. Rebecca and Trooper Nettles went out to the police car then and I watched through the window as he strapped on his belt. I saw the gun glittering in the moonlight. Then they left.

By this time I could see about a half dozen figures out in the fields with lights. They were some of the neighbors and Uncle Ike, Dad, Amos, and Danny Biller. Dad was looking behind the bushes in the garden. I had no desire to help search as I thought she will be found without my help, and I wouldn't have wanted to find her myself. I didn't consider getting out of the house, but I was very glad that others were searching. People have asked us since if we didn't just call and call Naomi's name. No, we didn't call her name once—we hadn't considered it. In the back of our minds we must have felt there was no use to call.

The house was quiet again after everyone was out searching. The clock ticked loudly. Mary and I didn't know what to say to each other. I just sat at the table propping my head. Mary paced the kitchen and pretended to be doing something. Finally, I told her I was going over to

Mom, but would be right back. I just had to get out of the house! When I arrived at Mom's, in our house, she told me I should go back to Mary and not let her alone! I asked her to go with me because I felt afraid. Mom said she couldn't understand why Jean Tressler, our neighbor, didn't come. She wished she would. Then my brother Levi came walking in and asked about Naomi again. He could not understand what was going on. Mom wrote a note for Jean, asking her to come down, and sent Levi up to Tresslers with it. It seemed we groped for help, or even just a word of hope from anyone.

Then Mom and I walked over to Mary's again. Outside her door, before we went in, I whispered to Mom, "I have a feeling that something terrible happened to Naomi." I hoped she could give me a word of encouragement, yet deep down I knew she couldn't. She whispered back, "Don't tell Mary, but I think Danny Biller killed her." Just as she said it, I knew in my heart it was true! She spoke my thoughts, but having someone say it pierced my heart and a terrible feeling of dread flooded through me. I said, "Oh, Mom...."

Neither Mom, Mary, nor I sat down. We kept pacing from one window to the next. Soon Jean came down and she said she would have come sooner, but she didn't know what was going on when she saw the lights in the fields. She didn't realize it involved one of us. When she heard our story, she didn't say much, but I saw the look she gave Mom when she learned that Naomi had gone to the Biller home.... Mom then gave Jean several numbers to call and asked her to notify Amos Eshes. Jean said she would call and come back immediately.

Every time the door opened, we looked up hopefully, but there was no hope. By then we knew the fire company was out because we saw the trucks driving through the fields with high-powered spotlights.

Every direction we looked the fields were flooded with lights. People have told us since that those lights were seen for miles around.

I kept thinking to myself, "Why don't they just make Danny tell them where she is?" But again, I didn't realize the angles of the law.

In the meantime, the police kept an eye on Danny. By this time, there were about six police cars at the Biller home. Rebecca had to stay with Trooper Nettles all this time. After Dad had been out at the Biller home, Amos was also out. Neither of them entered the home, only the garage, but they both talked with Danny and his dad. Mrs. Biller was not at home. They noticed nothing out of the ordinary except the basket. Danny went outside with Amos to help search. Several of the neighbor men also talked with him and asked him if he had seen her anytime, and he always said he had not. It seemed he was mostly interested in knowing where the police were and what they were thinking.

As Rebecca said, it seemed time and again Danny would show up beside her when she was standing by the police car, while the officers were consulting with each other. One time she asked him, "Danny, have you seen my Aunt Naomi?" He told her he had not. Then she asked him if he didn't hear the freezer lid go down anytime either. He again said he did not. She asked him, "Are you sure?" He again denied it.

At one point, Trooper Nettles came to our house again and asked Mary more questions about Naomi. Then he asked her if she ever used the phone in the Biller home. Mary said she might have, but customarily she did not. We later learned that he asked this in case Hans Biller would not allow them to search the house when they would ask him. Even if he would have refused, they still would have had the right to search the house because of this, and they did not need a search warrant.

The police did suspect Danny's involvement all right, but they needed evidence of foul play before they could pin him as a suspect. So far it was just a a missing person case.

After the police thoroughly searched the garage, one of Naomi's glass lenses was found inside the garage door by a pile of rubbish. Both Dad and Amos had overlooked that. It probably was a good thing. Her glass frame was found behind the freezer, all bent up. It must have been then that about a half dozen officers held a consultation by Trooper Nettles' car in our field. Nettles came to Rebecca who was close by and said they want to have a talk with Danny. She told him he was here a minute ago. Then they saw him walking out our lane, so they got in the car and followed him out the lane and up the road and in the Biller driveway.

Nettles told Rebecca to stay in his car while he followed Danny into the garage. She waited awhile, then finally she got out of the car and looked around the house. She looked in the garage window and saw Danny up against the wall with his hands up, surrounded by five or six officers. She then walked back to the car and waited awhile yet. Finally, Trooper Nettles came to her, put his hand on her shoulder, and said he had something to tell her but she must remain cool. He told her, "We found your aunt, but she is not alive."

Rebecca looked to the ground and did not make a sound. He asked her if she understood, and she nodded yes. Then he went back in again. Just then Dad walked up to her and she told him what Nettles told her. I do not know what their reactions were.

Meanwhile, Mom, Mary, and I were still in the house wondering.... It must have been around 10:30 then. Finally, the door opened and Elam's two girls walked in. We were so glad to see someone. They wanted to know what was going on. I looked out the window and watched the searching. In the midst of the sounds of trucks, people, etc., I heard one low blast of the fire siren. Dimly, in my mind, I thought they must have found her now, but I didn't say anything to the others. They hadn't heard it. The sound chilled me.

Again the door opened and we anxiously looked to see who was there. It was Dad and Rebecca, and by the way they looked, my heart stopped beating for I knew they had bad news. We did not say a word as they stepped inside and stood by the door. They both covered their faces with their hands and sobbed. Rebecca finally said, "They found her." Dad finished it by saying, "But she is dead." The words dropped on us like a bomb.

I quickly glanced at them to make sure I heard correctly, then I broke into uncontrollable sobs and kept repeating, "No, no, no, not Naomi!" I got up, walked over to the desk to lay my glasses down. Rebecca must have thought I was getting hysterical for she took hold of my arm and told me to sit down. I quickly shook off her hand, laid my glasses down, and sat down again. Mom and Mary were both weeping heartbreakingly. We were like a wound-up spring letting loose.

I suddenly quit sobbing and started asking Rebecca questions. I wondered where they found her. She said she thought it must have been in the house somewhere. Mary covered her face with her hands and said, "How will we ever, ever get over this?" I looked around, thinking, "Can't someone tell me it's not true!??" But nobody could and I shook my head in despair. The reactions to such a kind of grief can never be described.

After our initial reactions, we started talking to each other and wondered and wondered about a lot of things, such as, "why," or "how" was she killed. And where was she found? Mary admitted then that she finally had wondered if maybe she was kidnapped when she just didn't return home.

As we were sitting there wondering what to do next, our two neighbor ladies, Jean and Betty, walked in. They had not heard the news but knew as soon as they saw us that something drastic must have happened. We all cried and cried again and they cried with us. Then Betty suggested that we pray. We all got up, formed a circle, and held hands while Betty prayed aloud.

It was exactly what we needed just then and was like a balm to our bleeding hearts. As she was praying, it was the first that I felt I could go on. I doubt if I will ever forget that prayer. Every time I see Betty now, I think of that moment and feel thankful.

We felt calmed down then (as much as anyone could under those circumstances). Betty and Jean left again to make some phone calls for us and came back with buns and coffee. One by one the three Huyards came—Ike's, Elam's, and Levi's. Words were inadequate. We later learned that Elam and Levi had both gone to bed after one of us had been there, asking if they had seen Naomi. They missed the search, and the next message they got was about Naomi's death. They simply had not taken it seriously and, of course, no one thinks of something like this.

I then wanted to go home to get dressed better, but I discovered I was afraid to go over by myself. Our household had something in common for a long time—we experienced a terrible fear. Even the boys felt it, but not as keenly as we girls did.

At one point, as we were sitting there, someone asked where Amos was. Someone said they think he went to use the phone. I almost panicked when I heard it and asked why anyone let him go alone! We had a fear of the dark and the unknown. It gripped us so much that we felt the need to be very protective of each other.

Sometime that night, a state trooper came and wanted two people to go along to identify Naomi's body. They would have liked someone from here to go, but Dad refused to go. Then Amos said he would go, but we told him he may not, as we had no idea what they would see and we did not want this imprinted in Amos's mind. Uncle Elam and Levi went along then.

After they returned, they did not say much, but they told us that they had her on a stretcher up on the porch. She was covered with a sheet up to her chin so they only saw her face. They said there was blood over her face and her mouth was open. We later learned that they needed two people to identify a body in case one of them dies before the trial, they still have one witness left.

The house was quiet that night. Mary did not want anyone outside the family notified that night except our bishop. Amos went over to tell the bishop's family. Around midnight, they came and had Joe Stoltzfus with them. We were so glad to see them, but what was there to say? We just shook hands and cried. Their presence brought us comfort. We needed comfort from anyone who could give it.

I guess it must have been around 2:00 a.m. when most of the people left for home and it became quiet. When we looked out the window at the Biller home, there were flashing lights from police cars out there all night.

Around 4:00 a.m., Amos, Rebecca, and I decided we would go home and try to sleep a little. I don't remember who stayed with Mary.

Most of that night Levi, the retarded one, was very disturbed. He did not help search, but kept going from our house to Mary's, asking where Naomi was. He must have gone to bed around midnight, not knowing that she was found, but every time someone opened our door, he got up and asked. No one really gave him satisfaction.

When the three of us went upstairs to go to bed, Levi got up and asked

18

us where Naomi was. We then told him that she died and he should go back to bed. He was thinking, as in deep thought; then he went back to bed.

I was thinking as I went to bed, "Here we are going to bed with a heavy sorrow while other people are probably sleeping as if nothing had happened." I was glad others could sleep, not knowing. But I know now that it is a good thing to share sorrow with others because with others knowing, many prayers are sent up to God. (The very next day one could feel the prayers of others, and I guess that is the **only** thing that kept us going at one time.)

Rebecca and I tried to sleep but discovered that sleep was impossible, so we talked instead. Soon after we were in bed, we were badly shaken by a loud scream coming from the boys' bedroom. We jumped out of bed and ran over. Amos was lying in bed, staring at the ceiling. When we asked him what was wrong, he mumbled something about a dream, but didn't say more.

We went back to bed with chilled feelings. That was only the beginning of bad dreams for us. At one time, I hated to go to bed because I was afraid of the dreams I would have. They would wake me up.

— Chapter 3 —

Some of the neighbor men came and started the milking at 5:00 a.m. Bob Tressler came and took Amos to fetch two of our uncles who do not live in the immediate area. They also made other stops. Bob and Jean were godsends to us. Bob did a lot of running around for anyone involved over that time, and we later found out that at the place where he worked, they kept his gas tank filled all week free of charge. They wanted to help in some way.

At 5:00 Sunday morning, Jean also came down and picked me up to take me to tell David's and bring them home. I wanted to get there before 6:00 when they'd start out for church. On the way up, I kept thinking, "This is a bad dream," yet subconsciously I knew it wasn't. My thoughts seemed to be weaving in and out of it. I never hated to do something as badly as I hated to bring them this news. How I wished it wasn't true!

When we arrived, Esther was in the milkhouse. As soon as she saw us, she stared at us an instant, then she quickly asked, "What happened?" I avoided her question and asked her where David was. She told me and then she again asked what happened. I took her hand and started leading her toward David. She said, "You must tell me what happened!" So I calmly told her that Naomi had died. She didn't say much, but tears gathered in her eyes. When we got to David, Esther told him why we came. Jean and I glanced at each other behind her back. Suddenly she looked questioningly at us and asked the question which I dreaded, but knew she would ask. "What happened; why did she die?"

I did not answer, nor did I look at her, but I started to cry. She took hold of my arm and sort of shook me and asked in a frantic voice, "Did something happen?" I said, "Yes, it did. She was murdered." She gave me one frightened glance, then she reacted in the same way I had. She burst out in uncontrollable weeping and kept repeating, "No, no, no, not Naomi," shaking her head. I didn't touch her or try to stop her. David's face turned completely white and he didn't say a word.

Suddenly Esther quit crying and asked what happened and where. We talked about it for a few minutes, then they got to work to finish up their chores. Esther went out in the dark to the calf hutches to feed the calf and I was wondering to myself how she could go out there by herself. But she was acting on impulse, for later she also experienced a terrible fear the same as we did.

After David's and I arrived home, there were quite a few people there already. The uncles were making funeral arrangements, but it was difficult to decide which day to schedule the funeral for we had no idea when the body would be returned because of the investigation.

As we were discussing her death among us, one of our aunts said, "Now my dream makes sense." She then told us that about a week earlier she dreamed that she was in a deep, dark pit and couldn't get out or even see light. She was alone and afraid. Suddenly, angels appeared and were all around her. When she woke up, she was wet with sweat. She wondered what it could mean. As she told us this, she was crying and said that surely those angels can comfort us now. It was a nice thought.

In the morning, someone brought in a Sunday newspaper. On the front page, in large, bold headlines, it said, "Amish Woman Slain," and it went on to say that Naomi was the first Amish person in Pennsylvania to be murdered. It also showed a photo of Danny Biller. The sight of his face made us feel sick. He was eighteen years old. (If he had been only seventeen, he probably would have been tried in a juvenile court, and he might not have gotten a jail sentence.)

While reading the newspaper, I thought, "Yes, I guess it will be broadcasted." I had not thought of that yet. We little suspected then how very much it would be broadcasted all over the United States that whole year, following the hearings and trials.

Sometime in the morning, Amos called out to Dale Bair to go and tell Stevie. I guess we didn't realize the impact such news had on those of the family when they had not first known about the search, etc. Stevie thought it must be a mistake, or he didn't want to believe it, for he called back to Jean to ask what was going on. Dale then took him to sister Sara's home in Centre County. They were at church. Dale brought them home to us. It was a long ride home.

Mose also received his message at the mountains but didn't get the details. He had in mind the victim was one of his sisters. Someone drove him home then for he knew he was not in shape to drive himself. He said he was actually glad he was not home while the search was going on because he was sure he would have gone directly into the Biller home and searched it. That would have spoiled a lot of evidence for the police and could have ruined the trial.

He later told us that Trooper Nettles came out to talk to him and ask questions about the Amish people. Nettles wanted to know about the attitude of the Amish people in a murder case. Since it was such a rare happening for our people, the police were at a loss as to how we would deal with this. They were afraid we would not cooperate with the prosecutors and would not testify in court. This was very important to them, of course.

They were very relieved when Mose assured them that he knew

his family well enough to say that they would be completely cooperative and were not altogether naive as far as laws are concerned. We were only glad someone was doing something to get the right person locked up for everyone's safety. Revenge was the farthest from our minds.

We still had not heard in which part of the house her body was found until we read in the newspaper that it was found in the basement with sixteen stab wounds. That thought was horrible for us. And still, there were hundreds of questions going through our minds.

Sometime in the forenoon, Trooper Nettles came to our house and wanted to talk with Mary. He told us that Danny is a suspect and is locked up, plus a few more things. We asked him if he had suspected Danny the evening before. He didn't answer our question but said, "I knew him only as a thief and a robber." He told us Danny was a habitual liar. We later learned that the police are usually ninety-nine percent sure of a suspect before they dare arrest him.

Nettles did not tell us more details, nor did we ask, although there was so much we would have liked to ask. He then got Mary to go along out to his car to identify Naomi's dress. She did not take the dress out of the bag so she didn't see the condition of it. It was best that she didn't, for if she had, she would have seen it was slit open the whole way down the front.

A few news reporters came to our door several times that forenoon and wanted interviews. Mother went out to talk to them and told them we had no comments. For several weeks, different reporters came almost every day. We did not comment, but they went to the neighbors and also to the Billers and got satisfaction there.

That first Sunday forenoon it was quiet around here. People had not found it out too much yet and, also, our church district had church services. Most of the church people didn't hear of it until they arrived at church. The services lasted only somewhat over an hour. One of the ministers remarked to the congregation that no words were necessary that day. I am sure it was that way. In the afternoon, people were coming and going constantly. Practically everyone who came in the door that day, and also the following two days, wept unashamed.

Sometime during that Sunday, Andy Fisher, whose daughter had been murdered, came. He said his wife could not make herself come, as it made the memories too real for her. We were very glad to see him and talk to him. He was a big help to us and proved to be a true friend in the following months.

Andy Fisher gave us a pointer about talking to reporters, saying we should talk to the reporters because the public wants to know how we feel and they want our opinion. He said if the public gets stirred up enough about these senseless murders, maybe some of the lenient laws can be changed. It made sense and later on, some did talk to reporters.

Sometime toward evening, Hans and Leona Biller finally came in. It was a hard moment for us both. They cried and so did we. They said they are so sorry this happened. We told them it is not their fault and we do not blame them, asking them not to take it too hard. We felt so sorry for them, to the point where we forgot ourselves.

The Billers' minister and his wife had also come with them. The first thing that I heard the minister's wife say was, "As long as he's not proven guilty, he's innocent." I recoiled at those words and the rest of those who heard it did, too. None of us had said he was guilty. We learned later that the Billers hardly said anything or went anywhere after that without the aid of their minister. None of us knew the minister or his wife, and we never really did get to know them too well. Our hearts were heavy for Hans and Leona that evening. Mom and Leona had a nice talk together before they left.

On Sunday people were coming and going all evening. Finally, around 10:00, someone came in and announced that the undertaker was here. We were surprised to hear it. As they carried Naomi's body in, I'm sure our thoughts all corresponded—"What will she look like when they open the coffin?"

I thought I had prepared myself for a shock, but I was not prepared for what I saw. After the undertaker opened the coffin, several people gasped and I guess more of them wanted to. Some of the cousins started weeping loudly. The whole scene chilled me with a numbing effect. It seemed as if I was filled with a sudden anger mixed with a terrible sorrow. I thought as I looked at the body, "Her body is here, but her soul is gone."

In the midst of the weeping, Mary was standing back in the corner, silently weeping. Esther walked over to her and said, "Peace, peace. Naomi is at rest now."

Oh, how I hoped she was! I thought she would deserve perfect rest if ever anyone did, after what it looked like she had gone through.

Both her eyes had bruises around them. Her forehead was black and blue and her cheekbone was discolored also. There was a knife wound on her chin and on her neck. Her teeth were not in her mouth as the undertaker said they were broken in two pieces. We did not see the rest of her body because it was covered up. We did not ask how it looked either.

Before the undertaker left, Mary asked him if he could put make-up on her face or do something about how she looked. He said he would bring his kit along the next morning. When she asked him why he didn't put make-up on before he brought her out, he said his policy, when he worked with the plain people, was never to use make-up unless asked to do so.

It was probably around the hour of midnight when we got to bed, finally. I don't remember who slept with Mary, but I'm sure someone did. For me, to sleep by myself anymore was out of the question! I slept with Rebecca. I don't know about the others, but I slept very little that night.

On Monday, the neighbors and others came and did our chores, washed for us, etc. There were people in and out all day. When Mary first uncovered Naomi's face in the morning, it looked still worse. She covered it again, thinking, "We cannot have a viewing for her." But when the undertaker came and was done applying make-up, she changed her mind. He came every day until the funeral to apply fresh make-up.

As we were dressing Naomi's body, we had to be careful not to touch her too much, and we were asked by the undertaker not to lift her body. We cut her dress and cape through in the back and just laid them on, tucking them underneath her. Her whole chest was stuffed with cotton and bandaged shut. We later were told that the undertaker described the condition of her body to one of our ministers. He said her whole body was black and blue from head to foot, and it looked as if someone had stumped around on her, wearing hard-soled boots. Her jaw and nose were broken and her chest was covered with stab wounds, with one stab wound in the back. He said he never saw anything like it before, and he hopes he never will again.

At first I was hesitant to get near her body, as the whole thing nearly made me sick just thinking about it. Finally I decided I must, or it will never seem real. I stroked her hair which I had combed so often. Her face had a sad expression. Then I thought of Grandma and was very glad she did not live to face this. On Monday evening the house was very crowded. We were told later that there was a waiting line outside at one time.

Esther stayed overnight with us. She, Rebecca, and I slept together because neither one of us wanted to sleep alone. We were so tired that we simply had no choice but to sleep. Sometime during the night Esther woke me up and wondered if she may sleep between Rebecca and me, instead of on the outside. That is how afraid we were. Mary did not seem to be as badly affected that way as we were, but she did say, "It's not the dark we're afraid of. It's 'people' in the dark."

I think possibly if others heard of our fears, some might have thought we were being superstitious and not trusting enough. But I will say with first-hand experience that it takes more than trust. The mind tells you to trust, but the body is too numb and hurting yet to do that. It must take its course. In the meantime, it is **very** important to have people around. It is very unwise to force yourself to be alone and to "trust" until your body feels healed and you can handle it better. It might not affect all people this way. Some might not experience such fears, although I doubt very much if that is possible for family members. Anyone who forces himself to overcome fear immediately following such an experience is asking for a mental breakdown.

On Tuesday our house was literally rearranged when preparing it for the funeral. Everyone was very, very helpful. We did not keep track of how many people were in and out on Tuesday again, but there were many. All the non-Amish neighbors came in to view Naomi. Five couples came at one time.

Everyone of them said they feel she gave her life for someone else's, as it was bound to happen to someone eventually with the type of character Danny was. They had been afraid for themselves and their children. They did not trust Danny at all. They then told us that after a search in the basement by the authorities, a homemade sword was found, made out of sawblades. It chilled me to hear it!

I felt, too, she might have given her life for me, for I went out to the freezer more often than the other women around here.

Why did it happen to her? I wondered at the thought.

If it had been me, would I have been ready? Had I really accepted the blood of Christ as an atonement for my sins? Had I really accepted Him as my Savior? Did I really trust His promises for all those who acknowledge Him, and then love Him enough to keep all His commandments in exchange for what He did for us? Did I believe that "Hope" is a sure anchor for the soul? (Hebrews 6:19)

Did I really believe that hope will not disappoint us, as it says in Romans 5:3-5: "...But we glory in tribulations also, knowing that tribulation worketh patience; and patience, experience; and experience, hope. And hope maketh not ashamed; because the love of God is shed abroad in our hearts by the Holy Ghost which is given unto us." I believe for some of us it takes deep experiences to bring us to the knowledge of what Christ did for us. I believe Naomi's life was possibly taken as a sacrifice for this purpose.

I remember thinking, "If ever a person's faith in God is tested, it is now. It seemed illogical that such a thing could happen to someone who believed in God and His protection. Then what is the use of praying?" Even behind locked doors at night, my thoughts were, "Why try to protect ourselves if God will still allow such awful things to happen?" Even if there was danger, what would be the use to ask God for help? Naomi probably asked, too, and didn't get it.

26

Then, finally, I even wondered for an instant if there truly is a God. Are we all being deceived into believing something that isn't real? It was a dark, dark thought.

Finally, I had to stop thinking, as the whole thing was too deep. But one thing that was a good answer for us was when we asked a good friend of ours where he thought God was when this happened. He answered us with the question, "Where was God when His own son was killed?" It was a new thought.... I don't think He planned this, yet apparently for some unknown reason He allowed it.

It wasn't long until we felt that the hand of God was there, even if He allowed it to happen. One incident that verified this was when the police told us that in every murder case there are many loopholes for the murderer to get out, but in this case they will plug every one of them! They said they seldom get a case that is so clean-cut, meaning that the body was found within twenty-four hours, plus a suspect was locked up.

This all proved to us that the devil had power first-hand while Naomi was being attacked. Then when we first realized she was missing and prayers went up to God, the Lord God took over and the devil had to flee. The case was clean-cut then. Her body could not be disposed of as was planned (by the devil's power), of which I will write about later. Her body was found and Danny had no escape. It was soothing to us to know that the murderer was not running loose anymore.

I guess it affected others that way, too, more than we realized. One of the church women said she was afraid to go outside after dark. She said it was so unhandy to feel that way and she hated it. She said her husband could not feel for her at all, but tried to understand. It actually felt good to us to hear that we were not the only ones who felt this way.

An old, non-Amish man who lived by himself close by was discovered one day sitting on his chair with his rifle on his lap. He said, "They won't catch me like they caught that Amish girl. I'll shoot them!" It affected other people's children, too. Some were afraid to walk to school. When children asked their parents what happened, after hearing things in school, the parents hardly knew what they should say.

Our young minister's wife said her children were afraid to walk to school until she told them that the police have locked up that bad boy. In their innocence, these trusting children did not realize that there were others out there just like Danny Biller. Their mothers did not tell them. The oldest boy then said, "Those police are good people. I believe they will all go to heaven!" She later told this to Nettles and Detective Henry and it pleased them. They said they did not often hear things like that; often they are called the pig police.

The neighbors were all good to the Billers, too, in spite of the circumstances. For a few days they brought meals to them.

We later learned that Leona Biller called Jean Tressler one day and asked her if she would come and clean up the blood mess in their basement. Jean did not let on to her how shocked she was at such a request, but she told Leona, "I can't do that for you! Naomi was one of my good friends." She told her the fire company does voluntary work like that. We never found out who cleaned it up for her.

—— Chapter 4 ——

Wednesday was the day of the funeral, and it was a rainy day. We did not mind the rain because it matched our spirits. Rain made everything appear sad, but sunshine would have seemed mocking. We ate lunch around 10:00, before the services began.

When our Bishop got up to preach, everything was deathly quiet. He spoke so meaningfully. He said Naomi's death was truly a warning of how quick and unexpected death can occur for any of us. He spoke in his quiet, halting voice. He said surely she didn't realize she was walking towards her death as she walked out the lane....It seemed like a lamb led to be slaughtered, like Jesus himself.

I had to think, "If she would have thought that her death might be a help for even just one soul to gain eternity in Heaven, and she would have known she would have to face death in such a way, would she have walked out the lane and faced it? Would we be willing?"

Isn't that exactly what Jesus did for all of us? It put a new light on His death for me. The Bishop also said he thinks her life was spent like Paul in the Bible. She had no children of her own, yet she had many children. Almost everyone knew she was close to her nieces and nephews. One's thoughts travel far when sitting quietly under a sermon. I pictured Naomi going through her life, always being, more or less, shoved around, being the youngest and never married. She had to endure things many times, even up until her very end. It made me weep. And I believe she is even now having her reward in heaven for it all.

The other minister who had the main part in the services was John Lapp (who was eighty-five), one of our district ministers. He also spoke very fitting and it made us feel so close to him. He repeated the words of Solomon in the Bible, "Too much weeping weakens the body, and will not bring back the dead." But he wept, himself, while he said it.

As we stood beside the coffin, just before the undertaker closed it again, Esther whispered to me, "Do you think she is holding our baby Johnny now?" I thought she might be. The undertaker then turned around, glanced at me, and handed me the shroud which had covered her face and asked if I would take care of it. I hesitated an instant before I took it. I wondered what this is supposed to mean, and I shrank from it. But I took it and put it in my dresser drawer.

Stevie took the horse and buggy to go to the cemetery and took Rebecca, Mary, and me along. Going out the lane, we saw a TV News van and several cars lined up along the road. They had their cameras set up at different angles. As soon as the first teams were on the road, the cameramen jumped in the cars and raced down the road ahead of us and got us again at the next corner. This procedure followed until we turned in the lane to the cemetery. They did not go on any private property, as taking pictures without permission on your property is against the law, we were told. They knew we would not give our permission and they were respectful about it. The following days, in the morning and evening papers, the front pages were covered with photos and articles, as they had been since the first night. I had to think, "All this is about our Naomi who hated publicity."

At the cemetery, there was a non-Amish man among us who was a complete stranger to us. No one seemed to know who he was. It was our belief that he might have been a reporter who understood German or maybe had a recorder on him. We never did find out who he was.

When we came back from the cemetery, our house was back in order again. It was such a good feeling to see everything back in its place again and supper waiting for us. The church people and neighbors did a lot of work those four days. We feel we can never repay their kindness. The best way to repay such a kindness is to pass it on when the need arrives. The evening of the funeral was the first quiet evening we had since the happening, although we had company.

On Thursday, December 2, we all walked to the wedding at Uncle Levi's where their Annie was married. It was a sad day instead of a joyful one for all the Huyards. It was very hard to face everyone. Naomi had looked forward to that wedding very much! The Bishop preached a very fitting sermon. When he came across the story of where Abel was slain by Cain, it brought tears to our eyes. An innocent person slain and then hidden by the murderer...but the blood cried from the earth. And God heard. I just couldn't help it. I had to weep during most of the sermon. We didn't stay late in the evening.

Our mailbox was full of mail that day. Uncle Ammon's came home with Mary and stayed overnight. The next morning they left for home. We were asked many times if Mary sleeps alone in her house at night. So far, it seemed as if we were taking an hour at a time and had not too many thoughts on the future.

On Friday morning, my driver came to take me to work. I had forgotten about going to work. I told him I didn't feel like working today. In our minds it seemed as if everyone else's life had changed, too, like ours had. It seemed as if everything around us should stop, too. Yet, we soon realized that the rest of the world was passing by as usual. Traffic was going as usual, people laughed and joked, and we knew we'd join in sometime, too. But at the time we couldn't see our way through at all.

The thought of going away to meet people was far back in our minds. I had no desire to go anyplace. We were just glad that people came to see us.

On Friday forenoon, I noticed a well-dressed gentleman talking with Amos out on the lawn. I did not trust anyone, but Amos was very trusting, so I went out to see what he wanted. He shook hands with me and asked my name, then started asking questions concerning Naomi's death. I soon realized he was a reporter and he verified this by saying he was from New York and he wrote for *The New York Times*. He wanted to write an article.

I shivered when I realized he had my name. I did not want my name and address published in New York, as I imagined some bad guys looking me up and maybe doing something rash to make a name for themselves. The imagination stretches far at such a time. I asked the reporter to promise me not to mention my name. He hesitated, but seeing I was really in earnest and afraid, he shook my hand and promised.

Approximately a week later, we received one of his magazines and he was true to his promise. We also received articles from different magazines from friends of ours in other states. We were told it was publicized all over the United States in magazines and on television.

All of New Holland was shocked over it and most people were outraged at such a senseless murder. A lot of people in New Holland had known Danny Biller and his character and were exasperated that nothing was done about him until something drastic happened. But everyone's hands had been tied, even the police, until he was caught in the act. They could only give him short jail sentences on his counts of robbery; then he was out again. Danny's last jail sentence had been six to twenty-three months and he was released on good behavior at five months, unknown to us. He was only home three weeks when this happened.

Many people were afraid that since this happened to someone Amish, we would be so willing to forgive that we wouldn't be concerned about Danny being locked up. They were mistaken as we were very concerned about this and certainly wanted him locked up and taken care of by the law. It made us feel so thankful for the police and all who took care of this. The people I worked for were very glad to hear me speak that way.

But now everyone was extra precautious about Danny's brother, Raymond Biller. Upon inquiring, we learned he was admitted to the psychiatric ward a few days after this happened. When the murder occurred, Raymond was living with his sister. When he learned about Danny, that same night he went out with his knife and was going to kill someone the first chance he got, as he did not want Danny to be ahead of him. When he got no chance to do this, he got scared and turned himself over to the authorities. This was a relief to everyone for the time being. I am convinced it is like an officer told us: "We cannot know what thieves and murderers are thinking, because they do not think like we do."

Mary did not go back to school that Friday either. She did not go back until after New Year.

That first Friday was a desolate day for us. I had my vocational class of fourteen-year-olds in the afternoon at our house. I later learned that some of the pupils did not want to come because they were fearful. I guess it was worse for them since they knew Naomi personally. I was used to having my class in the aunts' kitchen and Naomi would usually walk in the door as we were singing. Then she would help us. I guess this made more of an impact on them than I realized.

The undertaker came to see Mary sometime that Friday. He wanted to know more about the happening. Then Mary questioned him and now, two years later, this is still her question: "Where were our guardian angels we were taught to believe in??" I doubt if he had an answer for her. But after she was through telling him about how she had gone out to the freezer to see where Naomi was and had seen a figure at the doorway, he told Mary, "Don't you ever lose faith in your guardian angels. They were all around you!"

Probably they were.... He then told how he prepared an eighty-year-old grandmother for the grave the day after he did Naomi. He said there was no question about the old lady's death. Her work on earth was done so she passed on. But here, he said, are a thousand questions.

Yes, we wondered about a lot of things. What was the object for the killing? Exactly where or how was she found? We wondered what time she actually did die.

It is the Amish tradition to stop the clock at the time of a death in the family and keep it that way until after the funeral. In this case, Mary said, we would not stop the clock for we did not know what time it was when Naomi died. And I guess we didn't want to know.

Then on Friday morning, when Mary got up and looked at Naomi's battery clock in the kitchen—the clock had stopped...! This clock had never stopped before, to our knowledge. Naomi always kept it supplied with new batteries. The clock showed 5:50. Was this a coincidence? It was hard on Mary and us. If this was the actual time of her death, we knew she suffered much longer than we wished to think she did. Yet we knew it could be logical, for we knew it was about 5:00 when she left the house.

Still more of our questions were: Did she know she was being attacked? Did she have time to pray? How long did she need to suffer? We tried to convince ourselves that she was attacked from behind as she was bending over the freezer and it probably was over quickly. We decided Danny was filled with a sudden passion to kill. This made sense to us since we didn't know more details.

This was one main reason for our fear of being alone. How could we tell that someone would not sneak behind us sometime and kill us, too? We mistrusted people now. Dad admitted to Mom that he hated to work in his broom shop anymore for he had to work with his back to the door and there was only one door. He had the feeling he must be looking over his shoulder constantly.

I quit working at my jobs where I had been working alone. I knew without trying that I couldn't take that. Mary wasn't convinced that Naomi was attacked from behind and that it was over quickly. She was afraid she was trapped as soon as she was inside the garage because her one glass lens was found just inside the door. In our hearts we knew it could likely have been that way, but we didn't want to think it.

Another question in our minds, too, was, "Why was her glasses frame then found behind the freezer when her one lens was found inside the garage door?" It may have seemed foolish to others why we even cared to know about these things, but only those with similar experiences will understand.

It is only human to wonder...and so much easier for those not involved to shove it aside and think logically about it.

On Friday afternoon, a well-dressed gentleman came to the door. When he was invited to come in, he pulled out his badge and introduced himself as Detective William Henry from the Ephrata Police Barracks. He said he was working on the case and asked a few questions. If we thought we would finally get answers to some of our questions, we were disappointed. He politely answered what he could though. Later, after we learned more about the police and their ways, we learned that in this case they knew lots of facts from the first night on, but they didn't tell us.

Henry was a handsome man, quiet spoken, and a perfect gentleman all around. He said before he left that we would be seeing lots more of each other. This proved to be true. We learned to depend on him as a true friend, aside from a detective. We later learned that it was no accident that he was sent out that Saturday night, but that the police do their best to send him out when a murder case turns up. When we asked him where he was that night, he said he was there (at the Biller home). Rebecca told him she didn't see him. He quietly replied, "I was there." As we learned to know him better, we learned that he has a way of melting into the shadows.

On Saturday there was company in and out most of the day and overnight. On Sunday we also had company in and out all day—more than eighty people till the day was over. Someone stayed with Mary overnight, too. The following week there was company here every evening, plus during the day. In fact, for three months, there was company here every day, either during the day or evening.

—— Chapter 5 ——

It was probably within the third week that Trooper Henry came again and with him was Richard Sheetz, appointed to be District Attorney in this case. Mr. Sheetz was a young man with a lot of fire in him, but he was also very respectful. This time we had more of our questions answered.

Mr. Sheetz informed Mary and Rebecca that they would have to testify as witnesses at the hearing . Rebecca had to testify since she was the one who had called the police. We were told a hearing is followed within thirty days after a case arises. The reason for a hearing is the case is presented in the presence of the district justice. He then decides whether the case should go to court or not. Also, both attorneys get the chance to ask questions of the witnesses present in order to clear the case.

Oh, we had so much to learn that we did not know! We were also shocked to learn that the defendant (Danny) would be present at the hearing. The police said there is a reason for that. If the defendants were not allowed to be present at their own hearings and trials, they would imagine the attorneys would be lying about them and they would think they would be treated unfairly. This way they know what is going on. It then made sense to us.

Mr. Sheetz wanted Mary's story of Saturday evening, November 27. Bit by bit they went over the whole painful story. He wished so much that Mary could describe the figure better that she saw at the other end of the breezeway when she had gone out to check on Naomi. He questioned her so much about that. She told him she just mainly saw the figure's back and it was dark. But she thought it was a girl with flying, wavy hair. We soon understood that they knew it was no girl.

They told us more of what was going on at the Biller home when Naomi was found. We wondered why Danny did not take off and hide that night instead of staying to help search. They told us that he really had no choice because his dad had come home around 6:00 while Danny was still in the house. For him to try and escape after that would have made him look guilty automatically. He was smart enough to realize this. Finally, we summoned enough courage to ask where her body was found and who found it. They said Trooper Nettles found her in a spare room in the basement. They did not say more and we did not ask more.

They wondered if we had a regular pattern to go out to the freezer and also if the same person always went. They wondered if we ever talked with anyone when we went out there or if we ever went in the house. We said we seldom saw anyone out there, except occasionally Leona would come out and chat a few minutes if she heard we were there. It seemed she was lonely. I said I was in the house on different occasions and also in the basement, but Mary did not think that Naomi was ever inside the house while the Billers lived there.

They wondered if Danny ever made any advances toward any of us girls, or ever asked us any insuating questions. We said he never did for we hardly ever spoke with him since he was out of high school. They asked when was the last time he was at our farm that we remember, and we thought he must have been fifteen when he was here one evening to sell cookies for school. He told us how his brother Raymond was in a reformatory school after being in so much juvenile trouble. We told him he surely wanted to do better than that. Then he said he wanted to be a policeman. Knowing his character, we knew he'd never achieve that goal, although we did not tell him.

Mr. Sheetz wondered if we ever had thieves in our home. We said we didn't, and he asked if we ever noticed any of our clothing missing, like underwear. We were almost too shocked to answer, but we said none were missing, to our knowledge. They also asked if any of our white aprons were ever missing, the same type of material as our head coverings. This was a real shocker. We said we had none missing, unless one of our discarded ones was missing. We did not ask why they asked these questions, but we knew they had their reasons.

Rebecca finally asked what we all wanted to know. "Was she—?" Sheetz said, "No, but—" Then he glanced at Henry and I saw Henry making a face at him. We wondered about his "but," but we did not ask. It was Henry's way to ease things for us, to tell us a little more each time he came. He was very gentle, and I guess it was good he was.

A hearing was scheduled for December 7 at the District Justice office in Blue Ball, but plans were changed later because of all the publicity and being afraid of violence from the outraged society. The hearing was then scheduled for December 22 in the Lancaster Courthouse.

Meanwhile, mail and company was a regular factor around here and appreciated so much. It was very good for us to receive letters telling us when they last saw Naomi and what she was doing. One letter writer stated how she remembered seeing Naomi at a wedding several weeks prior to her death. She said Naomi was singing lustily when she walked out the door on an errand and she was still singing when she came back in. It seemed to bring her so close again. I never before realized how such descriptions can be so soothing to the bereaved family. I hope I will remember that whenever I send out letters of sympathy to others in the future.

36

Experiencing death of loved ones is hard, but if it's not good for any other purpose, it gives you a sincere feeling of sympathy for others who also experience it. Yet, often those with the most experience have the least to say. Nevertheless, the "feeling" is felt. One thing that I hope I will never say to sorrowing people right after a death is, "Now your loved one is gone and you cannot change it, so you must lay it aside—start over." This is not sympathy! It is too soon to expect yourself to adjust to that right away. A listening ear from a person who sincerely wants to hear your story works wonders.

It seemed we groped for comfort from any source we could find. It gave us a despairing feeling if anyone tried to tell us we must forgive and start over. Underneath our numbed minds we knew that had to come yet, but it was expecting too much to start over now. The mind and body do not work that way. They need time to adjust.

At times I really felt like expressing myself, but then I would sadly think, "They do not understand!" so I sat back and refrained from talking. But, when Andy Fishers came, and they came often, we all expressed exactly how we felt. Naturally, when company came, people would ask a lot of questions. Sometimes we were so tired of even just thinking about it; yet it seemed we always wanted to talk about it. We felt best to get it off our chests. It was harder for us when others avoided the subject in our presence because we knew they were still thinking about it.

We received a letter from an unknown non-Amish person whose daughter had been murdered. She wrote, "Do not hide your feelings, and beware of remarks you might hear, such as—'She really handles this well.' Hearing such remarks, you subconciously try to live up to it, thus bottling all your true feelings. In doing this, you are heading straight for a mental breakdown. Grief is a lonely thing and may not work out too well if kept to oneself."

People would ask us if we do not get tired of company, and if we wouldn't want to be left alone at times. "No, No!" we'd say, "We need people!" I am sure others will never know how much we needed them. This was verified to us one evening in January. We and Andy Fishers went to visit a young Weavertown couple whose brother had also been murdered. He had been a truck driver and was killed by a hitchhiker. We noted the sadness in their eyes and they expressed themselves with our exact words, "We need people!"

So far, we did not have time to really concentrate on trying to forgive Danny Biller, as some might have thought. That wasn't our main problem. Everything still looked confusing to us. Our main thoughts were "**Why** would he do such a thing?" And then again we wondered, "Why didn't God prevent it?" Then someone mentioned a story of a father who tried so hard to figure out why his son was killed until finally someone told him, "God's thoughts and ways are as much higher than ours as Heaven is from earth, and you are trying to figure out His ways!"

One evening, soon after the incident, we had company which none of us have yet forgotten. We had known them, but they were not close friends. The man was an interesting person and asked a lot of questions about the happening. Just before they left, he starting telling stories about his elderly neighbor man. They were funny stories and just the way he related them made us laugh.

We laughed quite a bit that evening. It was soul-refreshing to find ourselves laughing again after we had thought we never could again. Now, every time I see this man, there seems to be something special about him. He apologized for being funny that evening, but he need not have bothered.

Those first weeks my mentally-retarded brother Levi did a lot of thinking. He seemed to be pondering Naomi's death. He asked Mom, by pointing to his heart, if that is why Naomi died. Mother nodded yes. Another time he was studying the front-page picture of the newspaper where Naomi's basket was sitting on top of the police car. Still another time, when we were in the kitchen discussing some of the details, we suddenly noticed Levi sitting by himself in the living room in the dark. He was leaning forward, listening intently to our conversation. Finally, we decided he must have gathered the story.

Many groups of Christmas carolers stood outside our house and sang. This was very beautiful, but it made us cry. Most of them also stopped and sang at the Biller home.

It was always Mary's schedule, as far as I remember, not to go to bed till around 11:30 to 12:00, so having company in the evening suited her fine. Even after her company left, it was still not her bedtime and we could not make ourselves go home and let her by herself. So Rebecca and I sat up with her until her bedtime; then we'd go home to our bed. She said she was not afraid to sleep by herself, for which we were very thankful. She had a lot of courage. The boys would also occasionally take their turns to sit up with her. Often, when we did go to bed, sleep would not come. Other times we were so tired we were forced to sleep. When I think back to that winter, I wonder how we survived with such a lack of sleep. I'm sure we had reserve energy.

We all noticed that whenever we opened Mary's door, she would turn around swiftly to see who was there. This was something which she had not done before. It seemed our imagination played more tricks on us when we were real tired. It is a fact that when your body is physically exhausted, your mentality will be affected also.

Sometime before the hearing, Detective Henry came again. Mary asked him if there was anything he could do to prevent all the publicity in the papers. He said they could not put the lid on, but he would see what he could do. We later learned that he somehow persuaded the editors of the Lancaster newspapers not to publish any photographs. We did not know how he did it, but through all the hearings and trials, no photos were published of any of us, or any other Amish people, although many were taken. However, there were many printed of the defendants, attorneys, and the other witnesses, and of our farm buildings.

Before Detective Henry left one evening, he suggested that we try to look forward to Christmas, in spite of everything. Mary broke into sobs and said, "Things go on as usual in other homes, but here—Naomi just isn't here anymore." Henry was very sympathetic.

—— Chapter 6 ——

On December 22, the hearing was held in the Lancaster Courthouse from 9:00 a.m. to 4:00 p.m. All the seats in the courtroom were filled. Everything became quiet when Danny walked into the room with his quick, cat-like walk and took his seat beside his attorney. He had his back turned toward the audience and sat facing the witness stand, like the defendants usually do. He actually looked worse than he did in his photos. His wavy blond hair hung down below his shoulders and his eyes had a vacant, haunted look. He sat motionless throughout the whole ordeal.

We all later admitted to each other that we had a sudden feeling of anger inside us when we saw Danny. One of my brothers said he felt a strong urge to jump over the seats and grab hold of Danny's long hair and bang him around until he told the truth! This was exactly how we felt. We had to fight against the feeling. We thought, "Here the attorneys are asking the witnesses all these questions to try and clear the case, while he sits there and could tell us all about it!"

Dr. Penades, the pathologist, was the first to testify. He described the condition of Naomi's body when she was brought to him. He had to describe in detail what each wound did to her body. The deepest stab wound was four-and-one-half inches. That was the length of the knife blade. He then went on to explain the wounds in her face and body, how the nose, jaw, and neck were broken. When the defense attorney asked the pathologist what instrument was used to do all this, he said it appeared to be a blunt object. He went on to explain how she had an abrasion all around her neck and a gag in her mouth. This chilled me to the bone! This is part of the pathologist's testimony which was printed in the newspaper:

> Three of the stab wounds were in Miss Huyard's neck, 10 were in the right side of her chest, two in the left side and one in the back, he said.
>
> The chest wounds, the pathologist said, caused the most damage, puncturing her lungs and heart.
>
> In answering a question by the prosecutor, assistant district attorney Richard S. Sheetz, Jr., Penades said he was able to determine the woman was alive during the stabbings because of evidence in her other organs.
>
> "When a person is bleeding to death," he said, "the body reacts to save the life."
>
> Two of the organs were without blood, indicating that they had tried to force the blood to the heart where it was needed. Her

stomach, he said, was filled with blood indicating she had swallowed blood while alive.

Penades said there were no marks on the woman's hands that would have showed she tried to defend herself against her attacker, but her face was covered with tiny red hemorrhages indicating she was suffocating during the attack.

When the defense attorney asked him what the actual diagnosis of death was, Dr. Penades said it was asphyxiation (suffocation) and bleeding to death. This was an awful blow for us. When the defense attorney tried his best to get an answer on certain questions, which he chose not to give real satisfaction, he answered his questions indirectly. He was a foreigner with a strong accent and very shrewd. One could tell that he was used to dealing with defense attorneys. When he was asked whether he had known the victim prior to this, he said he had not, but he knew she was Amish because she had the appearance of an Amish lady.

When Hans and Leona Biller testified, we were able to piece more of our puzzle together. Hans testified that he arrived home around 6:00 that evening and noticed nothing unusual. He thought he was alone in the house until Danny came up from the basement. They exchanged a few words, then Danny asked for a garbage bag. Hans didn't think to ask what he wanted with it, but he presumed he wanted to take the trash out, for he put the kitchen trash into the bag and left the room with the bag. He then later came up and got something to eat. Both of them went to the TV room in the basement and watched TV until my dad came to the door and asked if they had seen Naomi. Later, when the police asked permission to search the house, Hans gave his permission.

Trooper Nettles checked the upstairs and Hans walked with him. When they went to the basement, he stood in the doorway of the spare bedroom while Nettles looked around. He saw Nettles look under a blanket on the floor, but that's all he noticed. Nettles came out again and they both went upstairs again. He did not know until they were upstairs that Nettles had found her.

When Leona testified, she was an emotional wreck. She said she didn't know anything was going on at home while she was at work. Sometime around 10:00, one of the neighbors fetched her at work, but did not tell her what was wrong. She had in mind that maybe Hans had a heart attack. When she got home, she saw all the police cars and commotion, but still no one told her what happened. Trooper Nettles took her aside and showed her a paper bag with a knife in it. He asked her if she knew whose knife it was. She told him it was Danny's. The defense attorney was still trying to find a way out so he asked her how she could tell whose knife it was if it was in a bag. Leona repeated that it was Danny's knife. When asked if Danny carried it, she said he always carried it around in his hip pocket.

Trooper Nettles told us on the way home that the reason no one was allowed to tell Leona what happened that night before she came home was because he wanted her to first verify that this was Danny's knife. Being the mother, she might have answered differently if she knew some-one had been murdered. Police take every precaution.

When Trooper Nettles and Detective Henry testified, we were again in for a shock. Nettles testified that when he discovered the body, it was hidden under a sleeping bag, partially under the bed. It was nude, except for two black stockings. Her head was completely covered with a make-shift hood of white material, tied back with a purple material (which we knew had been part of her scarf). Her hands were tied in the back with a pair of pantyhose and a rope was around her neck. Hearing all this made us feel sick.

When Detective Henry testified, he said he got a call from Trooper Nettles, asking for help for a murder case in New Holland. He found the body as Nettles had described it. They then took fingerprints of the house and searched the basement. A knife was found hidden under the pillow. Naomi's clothes were found stuffed in a bag beside the body. There was no evidence of any struggle or blood anywhere else in the house except right where the body was found. The garbage bag, which Danny had asked his dad for, was found with a few items of trash in a chest in the same room as the body was found.

Henry testified that after he had read Danny his "rights" that Saturday night, he took him up to the barracks. He talked for about an hour. Danny told Detective Henry that he was not at home that evening until around 6:00; he was at the Turkey Hill Minit Market looking for a job and also at three other places. He said he walked to all these places. Detective Henry searched this out and the clerks all said they had not seen him. The clerks also testified at the hearing.

Henry told us on the way home that it takes a good liar to cover up a story without a snag somewhere. We also learned that one of the "rights" which are read to a criminal is that one has the right to remain silent. Danny would not have had to talk at all to Detective Henry at his inter-view at the barracks. Henry told us on the way home that Danny's lawyer was getting disgusted because he could hardly get anything out of him.

Raymond Biller was also at the hearing, which disturbed us pretty much. He was asked to leave the courtroom by an officer when Trooper Henry testified. Rebecca and Mary also testified. Their testimony was mainly what they had been doing that Saturday evening. When Mary

43

took the witness stand, I whispered to David and Esther beside me, "We must really pray for her that she says the right things and doesn't say anything she shouldn't." She sat up there and very calmly answered the questions. We couldn't see how she did it, though her face was a picture of sadness. Afterwards, Mary said she felt as if something was guiding her and she didn't feel it was her own strength. I'm sure it wasn't.

Different times during the hearing Defense Attorney Reese leaned over and whispered something to Danny and he answered back. Then Reese put his arm around Danny and patted his back. One of our uncles had a long talk with Raymond Biller out in the hallway. He later repeated the conversation to us. He said he feels Raymond is sincere and he wants to get hold of his life and change. We weren't as convinced by his talk as our uncle was because we knew Raymond too well.

The Billers offered some of us a ride home. I had planned on going with them until I learned that Raymond was also going with them. I changed my mind, but Dad went home with them. Raymond stayed at his parents' home overnight, which left us very uneasy. One of our neighbor ladies later told us that on the night before Christmas, a very cold night, Raymond knocked on their door when she was at home alone. She said she would have loved to let him in where it was warm, but she did not trust him. She just talked through the door, asking him what he wanted. He said he would like to call his sister, but his parents weren't home and all the doors are locked so he could not get in to use the phone. The neighbor lady told him she was sorry she could not let him in but she would make his call for him; she dialed his sister's number but no one answered. He turned around and left and the last she saw of him, he was walking towards New Holland in the bitter cold. Truly, "The way of transgressors is hard..." (Proverbs 13:15).

How can you help someone whom you feel might kill you when your back is turned? Some might say you need a strong faith, but I would say it can't be done by faith alone. You need to use good judgement, too. We are not asked to throw our lives away when we could take heed, or have a better choice.

We were told by Detective Henry that a week or two after Christmas, Raymond stole a car in Ephrata and was caught and put in prison. He said Raymond wanted to be there with his brother. They did not mind prison life.

Danny was scheduled to appear in court again on January 26 to either plead guilty or not guilty.

The night following the hearing I dreamed about Naomi. I saw her very plainly and talked to her. That was the first of many nights that I dreamed about her. I do not put much hold into dreams, but every time I see her in a dream it is a big help to ease the loneliness. Others have also had nice dreams about her and told us about them.

—— Chapter 7 ——

I spent a lot of time with my sister Esther that first winter. She and her husband lived on a farm away from close neighbors, and Esther felt that she simply could not be by herself so much and stay sane. The whole ordeal certainly tested one's mental capacity.

One day when I was at David's home, Rebecca called and wondered if I wanted to come home that evening for we were getting company from Ohio, namely Dora (Coblentz) Miller. As soon as she mentioned the name, I knew who she was talking about. Dora, an Amish lady, had had a bad experience almost thirty years ago when her husband was shot to death in her presence. We had heard about that story before our experience with Naomi, but our thoughts, when fleetingly thinking about it, always were, "That happened a long time ago way out in Ohio." Now, when she heard about this, she decided to come and visit us. I did not want to come home to see her. I was not sure that I would be able to handle hearing about one more tragedy and I did not want to hear about it. My imagination was too active without hearing more. Now, two years later, I wish I had met her. Or rather, I would like to meet her now. I would now be interested to hear her talk, which proves that "time" can at least partially heal such wounds.

Meanwhile, I am sure Hans and Leona Biller were having a rough time of it, too. I am sure we did not realize the feelings they were harboring. I guess they imagined that all the Amish people are now against them, plus many others, and this put them on the defense. They seemed to shoulder the weight of Danny's deeds on themselves. They had not come here since the Sunday they were here at the viewing.

One Sunday, Rebecca and one of her friends walked out to visit them. Rebecca said she did not feel like staying long, as the visit left a bitter taste in her mouth. The Billers said that they are receiving letters from people, telling them to try to get Danny to confess. They did not say it, but implied that they can hardly believe that Danny would do such a thing. Rebecca expressed surprise to them why they cannot believe it, and reminded Leona how she used to tell us she, herself, was afraid of him. Now Leona denied that.

Hans showed her a part of a letter from one of their Mennonite friends who had written that he overheard one Amishman express himself to the other, "I hope they keep that boy locked up and I hope he gets punished, too!" After Rebecca read it, Hans asked her what she made of such a remark. What did he think she would make of it? She told him that with the company that comes to visit us, we never once heard such a remark or anything similar to that. But we did hear many people expressing sympathy for the Billers. She could have told them that such a remark was mild compared to remarks that some of our non-Amish neighbors made. Two of them said that if they ever saw Danny again, they would shoot him! Many people remarked that Danny, plus his parents, were lucky this happened to Christian people because otherwise the Billers would have had to be afraid. No one will know the feelings we had to fight against when the tempter came.

After Rebecca's visit, we decided we would stay away from the Billers, for it seemed to antagonize them to see us. But we did not like it that way. We tried to overlook a lot and felt a deep sympathy for them because they were under a strain, but it gave us a queer, uneasy feeling when we discovered their thoughts.

There were others who cheered us, too. An article was written about the murder in some magazine in New Jersey. In it there were some comments that Naomi's Uncle David had made, stating how we can forgive the murderer, even if it opposes human nature to do so. We need faith and help from a higher source, he stated. This article had reached a prisoner in the New York penitentiary because Uncle David received a letter from him. He showed us the letter. This man wrote that he was in prison for killing three people in a moment of passion, two of whom he dearly loved. He wondered what kind of people we were that we could ever forgive a person for such a senseless murder. He left his address and wanted an answer. David did answer him.

On January 14, we started building a new porch between the two houses to connect them. It was too much of a burden to always be afraid to go back and forth outside after dark, and we always felt guilty going home and leaving Mary by herself at night. It did not take any persuading for Dad to build a connection. Neighbors and friends helped a lot and it was soon done. We all felt so much better after it was done. We set up a ping-pong table out there and often in the evening the cousin boys or friends came to play with us. Mary was glad to hear noise out there for then she knew she was not alone. Between games we would chat with her and drink coffee.

On January 26, Danny Biller appeared in court and pleaded "not guilty," but we were not there to hear it. Soon after that, Detective Henry came out again. Trooper Nettles also came out and wanted Mary to identify a few more items of clothing. Her worst fears were confirmed when she identified the underwear. They were not torn or cut, nor did they have any blood on them. This was very hard on Mary and she did not tell us about it right away. Her fears all along were that Naomi suffered more than we think she did. By now we were almost sure of it, too. By the looks of her underwear, we knew Naomi had been unclothed before she was stabbed. It was terrible to think about it. Her dress was cut open all the way down the front.

Since Danny pleaded "not guilty," a trial was scheduled for March 7. Detective Henry told us there was a chance that the trial would be postponed, for they often are. When we asked why it is that way, he said the defense attorneys stall for as much time as possible, yet the police and investigators have exactly ninety days after the hearing to get their things in order for a trial. The defense attorneys have years to investigate before they schedule a trial if they choose to do it that way. Their reason for putting it off as long as they can is they hope that after several years, the key witnesses will have forgotten some of the main details, or sometimes when a key witness is an older person, he dies before the case comes to trial. Then the case can be thrown out and the defendant is let loose.

We were to learn a lot more of the ways of the law and defense attorneys. Detective Henry explained to us that the United States is the only nation in the world where a defendant is presumed innocent until proven guilty. All the other countries they are presumed guilty until proven innocent. Why arrest anyone whom you presume is innocent? It was an eye-opener to us that America is the most lenient nation in the world, but the result is that it has the highest crime rate, too.

The reason for having defense attorneys started out with a good purpose. It was so that innocent people were not hung or killed, like in the old days, before they had a chance to prove themselves; however, it has gone way overboard now. After the defense attorney knows in his heart that his defendant is actually guilty, he still goes on defending him and does everything within his power to acquit him.

Should the law work that when the defense council has the real story and knows the defendant is guilty, they should get off the case and say, "You are guilty and you must now take our punishment and we'll let the judge finish it up." People wonder, "Where are the police? Why don't they try and have some of these laws changed?" But Henry told us that their hands are tied. The defense has too much power. He said, "We police wonder how they sleep at night."

Many times the police are involved a long time with lots of red tape, and risking their own lives until a suspect is finally apprehended, only to be set free after a short sentence, or none at all because the defense council might find miswordings or some loophole in the investigator's work. According to the law, a defense attorney must do his job to the utmost, or the defendant may turn around and sue him. It certainly gave us only an inkling of the job of a policeman or district attorney, which is one who works for the Commonwealth. They risk their own lives and give so much of themselves for the sake of us all. If the daughter, or wife, of a defense attorney was raped or killed, wouldn't he get the other side of the picture? Could they continue with their type of job? The police feel that if the defense council would urge the defendants to come out with the truth at their interviews before the time of the hearings, instead of giving them the impression that they will somehow find a way out for them, many defendants would break down and tell the truth. That is what our unspoken thoughts were about Danny and his parents.

Personally, we did not want Danny locked up out of vengeance, but we certainly did not feel it was fair to society to have him on the loose in his condition and we were afraid of him. My brothers were not afraid of him though. Stevie said if he would have known that Danny was home again, he would not have allowed any of us women to go out there by ourselves. It was a woman he wanted, not a man. But if he was after a woman, why was she killed in such a horrible way? It was still a puzzle.

We women, of course, did not go out to the freezer at all anymore. One Saturday evening, Mary needed something and wondered if one of the boys could go out for it. Stevie was the only one available so he said he would go. We did not want him to go by himself at that hour on a Saturday evening. Rebecca almost cried about it. He said he would take a baseball bat along, which satisfied us. Later, when Andy Fishers came to visit, Stevie admitted that it gave him a funny feeling to be in that garage by himself.

I guess it was sometime in January that we heard a rumor that one of the clerks from Rubinson's Store in New Holland had seen Naomi walk out the lane that Saturday evening, November 27. This really interested us because we did wonder if anyone had actually seen her walking. We made it a point to talk with her and ask about it. She said she was at work that day and had punched out at 5:00. She guessed it must have been a few minutes after 5:00 when she was coming down our road. She saw this person walking in the field, close to the road, carrying a basket. As she got closer, she recognized Naomi. She wondered to herself, "Where is she going with her basket?"

As she drove by, she waved at Naomi and Naomi waved back. She said she hadn't more than passed her when she suddenly was filled with a horrible, uneasy feeling. She felt danger and her thoughts were that something will happen with that girl. She had in mind that maybe a car will hit her. She turned around in her seat and looked back to see if Naomi was still okay. She saw her walking in the driveway toward the Biller home and everything was okay. She drove on and tried to tell herself that it was foolish to feel that way.

48

The next morning at church she noticed that the Huyards were on the prayer list. She wondered about this and asked someone the reason for it. She was told that Naomi Huyard was murdered at her neighbor's house. She told us she would have fallen over had she not sat down. She said to the lady who told her, "But I just saw her last evening!"

We then asked her if it might not be possible that the power of evil coming from the Biller home was so strong that it reached out to the road, and she felt it. She said that was exactly what her minister told her. It was very hard on her. We couldn't help but wonder if Naomi had felt that evil power, too. If she did, why wasn't her death prevented by God? A train of thoughts could go on and on....

Chapter 8

Sometime in February, Detective Henry came to talk to us again. We were discussing parts of the happening. Henry told us Danny wasn't making out well in prison. He was in solitary confinement, by his own choice, because he was being harrassed by other prisoners. He said even among thieves and robbers there is a certain rate of mortality and some of those prisoners were angered at Danny's cowardly act of attacking a fifty-year-old woman. Rebecca asked Henry why they did not just leave Danny with the other prisoners. Let him face his medicine.

Naomi probably had been afraid, too. Then Henry said quietly, "Two wrongs don't make one right."

He asked us if we ever missed any of our frozen goods. We did not know that we had ever really noticed anything. We did say that on the very Saturday that this happened, Mom was saying that she really can't understand why our hamburger is all gone already. She said she wonders sometimes if Danny Biller is stealing it and helping himself. We laughed at her for imagining something like that and said it would seem funny if he would steal from our freezer with his parents' freezer right beside ours. She ended the conversation by saying, "If he's that hungry, he may have the meat." Detective Henry made no comment after we told him this.

Henry asked us if it ever crossed our minds that Danny might have had an accomplice in the killing. We told him we never gave it a thought. We felt that Danny could have handled her himself because she was so lightweight and little. He again made no comment. After he was gone, we asked each other, "What did he actually want?" We decided he was trying every angle he could to solve the motive in the killing. We had a feeling that he knew more than he was telling us because we had come to understand his ways and also the ways of other policemen.

We thought about the possibility of an accomplice, but that really made no sense because no one else was around that evening except Danny and his dad. We expected to hear more at the scheduled trial which was March 7. We were eager to have the trial over so that we could finally try to lay these things aside and go from there. It was our only ray of light for the future.

On the evening of March 2, David and Esther were here and Mary also had other company. One of Stevie's friends was here and they were out on the porch playing ping-pong. Around 9:30 everyone had left except Stevie's friend and David's. David and Esther then went out and hitched up. I walked out with them, and as we were standing by the carriage talking for a few minutes, a police cruiser pulled in the lane. I walked over to the cruiser; an officer got out and asked me if this is where Amos Huyard's live.

After I told him it was, he said the Ephrata barracks had a call from Detective Henry from Fort Lauderdale, Florida, this evening. Henry told him to come out and bring us this message so that we did not have to read it as a surprise in the morning paper (very thoughtful of him). He said to tell us that he has arrested another suspect in Florida for aiding in the killing of Naomi. It dropped as a bombshell!

I leaned against the officer's car for support. After a few minutes I asked, "How did he get down there, and how do they know?" He said he knew no details, but Henry would come out and talk to us as soon as he could. I thanked him and he left. My first thoughts were, "I can't believe this. How many more will they arrest?"

After the officer had gone, Esther came over to me and wondered what he wanted. I knew if I would tell her, neither she nor David would sleep that night and they were so tired, so I gave her an evasive answer. She gave me a strange look but didn't ask more. I walked over with her to David and we talked about other things till they left. Then I ran back to the house, through the dark. Mom and Dad were the only ones in the kitchen.

In a daze I told them what the officer wanted. It was an awful blow! This was almost as hard on us as the events of that first Saturday night. We decided we would not tell Mary about it tonight yet because we knew there would be no sleep for her if she knew. We thought she may as well have her sleep tonight because we knew there would be many sleepless nights again.

I went over to Mary's awhile and Rebecca was also there. When I left for our end of the house, I motioned Becca, behind Mary's back, to come over with me. She got up and walked over with me and I told her about the officer's message. She burst out crying and we all had to cry and cry. Our worst fears were real. We knew she must have suffered at the hands of two who were possessed with demonic forces and this was almost more than we could bear. I went out to the porch where Stevie was playing ping-pong and sat down. I wondered to myself how he could play ping-pong when something so terrible was on our minds. Then I thought, "Of course, he doesn't know it yet."

Stevie looked at me questioningly and I motioned for him to quit playing. Then I told him the terrible news also. He remained completely silent, then asked, "How do they know? I wonder if it's true." Then he couldn't play anymore. This is how it affected all of us. We really wondered if it was true.

Upstairs we children talked a long time before we went to bed. There was very little sleep for us that night. I wondered if I would ever be able to enjoy the things in life that I used to enjoy. Everything looked so foreboding.

The following days the daily papers were full of the news again. The front page of the morning paper was full of it, plus a photograph of the new suspect. His name was Tom Anderson, age twenty-one. He had thick, long hair that reached to his shoulders, and also a beard.

In the newspaper we learned that investigators had Anderson as a suspect since late January, but couldn't pin him down until a few days ago. Last Friday, when Anderson learned that they would arrest him, he fled to Florida. On Tuesday morning, Detective Henry flew down and he and two plainclothes men met him at a campground and arrested him. The papers didn't have too many details. We wondered so much about it all and were eager to hear from Detective Henry.

This news brought lots of company again. About a week went by until Detective Henry came to see us again. He answered everything we wanted to know. We never saw him like he was that evening. His manner was as cool as ever, but his eyes were blazing as he told his story. The newspapers had stated remarks which the defense attorneys made, such as, "The police had known nothing about a second suspect until Danny started talking."

But this wasn't true, for Henry told us that they had known all along, since the night of the happening, that there were two involved in the killing, but they didn't disclose it to the public or the defense attorneys. The first lead they had was that they had found two pairs of gloves hidden with the knife. (This didn't come out to the public till the trial in November though.)

The second lead was a few days after the happening (before Naomi was buried); the police in Lancaster received a call from Anderson and they referred him to Henry. He told Henry they will find his fingerprints on that knife, but that is because he and Danny had been together on Friday evening, November 26, and were carving initials on a building in Lancaster. He told Henry that it wasn't Danny Biller who killed that Amish woman, but he doesn't know who it was.

Detective Henry did not pretend that this excited him too much. He casually asked Anderson what his name was and where he worked. He thanked him for his information and told him that they might get in touch with him again.

Henry said he kept in touch with him by going to see him at the car wash where he worked. Henry felt sure that this was the other murderer, but he could not pin him down legally until Danny spoke up. When

Danny realized that he could not lie his way out of this situation and his trial date was approaching, he got scared and knew he had to tell someone the real story.

Prisoners are allowed a visitors' list of five people. If you are not on their list, you cannot visit them, no matter who you are. Anderson had first been on Danny's list. One day he came in to visit Danny and before he left he told him, "Remember, I will pay through the pages of the book," meaning he will pay somebody to somehow kill him if he tells on him.

This scared Danny, but he finally spoke up to his inmate. He told him about Anderson. His inmate told him that he should talk to his attorney about this. Richard Sheetz, our district attorney, and Reese, Danny's defense attorney, had interviews with Danny in prison. Danny told them that he and Anderson had been friends all summer. Sometimes he stayed with Anderson for a week in Lancaster when he wasn't in prison. Sometimes Anderson would come to the Biller home with Danny. When Danny's parents weren't home, they would steal meat from our freezer and take it along to Lancaster where Anderson boarded. Sometimes Anderson would use the meat to pay board to the girl he lived with.

On Friday night, November 26, they were together in Lancaster. Danny said they were drinking most of the night. On Saturday morning Danny hiked home and went to his bedroom in the basement and slept until afternoon. Around 3:00 Anderson hiked out to Danny's house. They were again drinking and before he left, Anderson said he would like some groceries, meaning food from the freezer. They went out to the garage to get food from the freezer and were in the process of doing that when Naomi walked in.

The way we picture it, Naomi must have been inside the garage before she realized that they were there because when you walk up the driveway, you cannot see into the garage. You open a door into the breezeway and immediately to your left is a door, without windows, that opens to the garage. There is a step going down into the garage, so she was most likely watching her step. I suppose she was as surprised as they were.

She asked the boys what they were doing. They said, "Nothing." She saw what they were doing because she then told them if they put it back, nothing will be said about it. Again, it looked to us as if she did the only possible thing left for her to do. She was probably inwardly afraid, but pretended she wasn't by talking to them, and she probably knew if she would turn around and try to get out, she would never make it. She knew she was trapped!

Henry said the boys jumped Naomi and took her to the basement. He did not tell us details—if she was conscious or not on the way down—but when we asked him whether he thinks she was conscious in the basement, he was reluctant to say. He did tell us she spoke to them down there. He gave no details of the happenings in the basement, except that Anderson did the stabbing. He said she wasn't raped, but they tried to force her to do things (which I will not put on paper) and she resisted. Also, the things they did to her (which I will not mention) were worse than rape. When we asked how they can prove these things at the trial, he just confidently told us that they would have ways to bring it out. He said it was either Danny or Anderson that Mary saw at the end of the breezeway when she was out to look for Naomi. That is when Anderson must have decided to leave.

After Anderson had gone, Danny intended to drag Naomi's body over to our field, but before he got it accomplished, his dad came home. Danny then thought that maybe he could somehow dispose of her with the garbage bag, but he also gave up that idea. He couldn't get her out of the house without being seen by his dad because they had no outside basement steps. Hans Biller arrived home at approximately 6:00, which shows that she was at their mercy for almost an hour.

When investigators questioned Danny about their motive in taking her to the basement, he denied that he was in the basement at all. He said Anderson was the one who attacked her and then asked him for gloves, a rope, and his knife and took her down to the basement while he was making dinner upstairs. When they asked him why he did not go for help, he said he was scared. Henry said every time they interviewed him, he had changed his story.

At his interviews, Anderson also denied practically everything. He said Danny attacked her by himself and took her to the basement. He said Danny wanted sex with her because he could have no other women. It was very exasperating for the investigators until they finally got some truth out of both boys and mostly got the real story together. Henry said they tried to get Danny to admit that their motive in taking her to the basement was for rape. He kept denying it. Henry said he knew he was lying because by evidence they had seen elsewhere in the basement and his prior jail records, they knew Danny had sexual hang-ups.

Finally, one day, Henry said to Danny, "Danny, I don't want to hear one more lie out of you!" He said the defense attorney took a lie detector test on him and brought the results to Sheetz and Henry, telling them that Danny passed the test—meaning he said the truth when he said that he wasn't in the basement and didn't have rape in mind.

Sheetz and Henry then gave the same test to him twice. They looked at the results and said to Reese, "What do you mean, he passed the test? He flunked both of the tests!" When Danny realized that, he finally admitted that he was down in the basement and that he did have rape in mind. They finally got most of the puzzle together.

The police have to be very careful how they handle the defendants for fear of throwing out a case. Many times they are so frustrated they would love to knock or choke the truth out of them, but they dare not touch them for fear of the law.

Henry said they had tapped some of Anderson's phone calls which he made from prison. This is how they got some information of where he had been boarding and who his friends were. Apparently he also was in trouble with the law different times, and was also a streetrunner who lived with different people almost constantly. He would also hang around the New Holland Sales Stables and sometimes slept there overnight.

They both would have had homes to live in, Danny with his parents, and Anderson with his aunt in Lancaster, if they would have behaved. They didn't try to hold a job for any length of time. While Anderson was working at the car wash and Henry would come out to talk to him there, the other workers finally asked him why this policeman is coming to talk to him so much. He told them, "He's my friend." Telling a lie was very easy for both Anderson and Danny.

Sometimes, when they needed new clothes, they would hang around at the malls in the evening and hide themselves until all the clerks were gone and the stores closed. Then they would exchange their old clothes for new ones and stay hidden in the morning again until the store was busy and they could escape unnoticed. They were finally caught at this act. Danny had so many scrapes with the law that it would have been hard to keep track of them.

When we asked Henry how he tracked Anderson down to Florida, he gave us a short account, but he told us that these things which he was telling us were not for public knowledge. We could feel that he also knew more than he was telling us. He said Anderson somehow got wind of it that Danny was starting to speak to the investigators and decided he had to flee.

We never did learn how the police were tipped of his destination, but Henry worked on the case until he learned that Anderson had wired money to a certain campground in Fort Lauderdale, Florida. Henry flew to Florida, rounded up two other detectives, got an arrest warrant, and they hunted around until they got to the right campground where he had wired his money. Anderson wasn't there yet, but on the day he planned to meet his money, Henry and two officers were there to meet him. Henry said Anderson was in a state of shock to see him and asked him, "What do you want here?"

Henry told us that a lot of these young guys out there class the officers as "pig police" and they underestimate their intelligence. We all later admitted to each other that we certainly would hate to have

Detective Henry on our trail!

After they had arrested Anderson, they read his "rights" to him and took him to prison. In the first interviews they had with him, he denied everything. At the interview, a defendant has the right to remain silent. If he does decide to talk, the conversation is either recorded on tapes or written down by an attendant. This conversation is then signed by the defendant so that when it appears before court, the judge and jury will know that the conversation was not sneaked, as this is illegal. Danny preferred all his conversations on paper, but Anderson chose to have his taped.

Henry told us that no fingerprints were found on the knife, so they still did not have very much proof. When Anderson kept denying everything, Henry tried a scare tactic on him. He told him, "Heck, we found your fingerprints on the knife!" This seemed to worry Anderson and Henry could see he was at the breaking point. At an interview at the police barracks in Florida, he finally opened up.

Henry told us we would really like that officer who was in charge. He said he is a fine Christian man and he has a rare way with thieves and criminals. He had a Bible sitting on the corner of his desk.

Anderson looked at the Bible and asked the officer if he reads that book. The officer told him he reads out of it, as much as he can, every day. Then Anderson broke down and cried. The officer then gently asked him if he has something on his mind that he would like to tell him. He said he did, and when questioned, he finally admitted that he and Danny were together on Friday night, November 26, and on Saturday afternoon he hiked out to Danny's place. He admitted they were stealing from the freezer when the Amish girl walked in. He admitted Danny made the first move by saying, "Let's have some fun," and then attacked her. He did not admit to anything from there on, except that he asked for Danny's knife and started stabbing her. He said he turned into a madman. He then fled the Biller home and hitchhiked to Lancaster.

After telling the officers all this, he seemed to realize he talked too much and refused to tell them more. When he was sent to the prison in Lancaster, Pennsylvania, he did not cooperate anymore at interviews, but denied any involvement.

Rebecca said to Henry, "Okay, we can now understand that Naomi surprised the boys by walking in on them, and they had rape in mind when they took her to the basement, and Anderson turned into a madman when he stabbed her, but why was she fixed up in such a weird way with a hood over her head, etc.?"

The fire in Henry's eyes glittered and he asked us if we ever heard of Charles Manson. We said we have heard his name mentioned, but that is about all. He then told us that Manson was a cult leader who, along with his followers, killed seventeen women in 1970, until they were finally caught. (They are still in prison in California.) He said that Anderson idolized Manson, and Naomi's body was put up exactly as Manson left his victims.

One of the girls where Anderson lived at one time said that Anderson was always talking about Manson and he also read a book about him. The district attorney in the Manson case had written a detailed book on the court trials of these murders to prove to the public the real evidence in the cases, because some of the public had been skeptical to believe all the facts. Henry then got a copy of the book and read it. Rebecca also got one and read it. In it there were pictures in black and white of how the victims were found. They were identical to how Naomi was found—nude, a rope around her neck, and a hood over her head. I looked at the picture one time, but I quickly slammed the book closed and never looked at it again. The book had been written with a good purpose behind it, but Anderson chose to devilishly demonstrate it.

—— Chapter 9 ——

On April 6 a hearing was scheduled for Anderson. Rebecca and Mary were not asked to testify this time, but we were urged to attend the hearing and to bring our friends along. The hearing was again held in the Lancaster Courthouse. Andy Fisher took some of us in.

It appeared as if Anderson might have had friends because several girls and a boy were present on his behalf. When everyone was seated in the courtroom and the doors were closed, everything got suddenly very quiet. We knew Anderson would soon be brought in. It was a moment which we all dreaded, yet we wondered what he actually looked like.

Soon two officers walked in the side door with a figure walking between them who we knew must be Anderson. He came swaggering in the room, his long hair swinging, a full beard, and walked to his chair with his head held high. He was also lightly built with quick movements. As he took his seat, he glanced back at the boy who seemed to be his buddy and gave him the "thumbs up" signal. Mary gave a short gasp and burst out in sobs. Rebecca, Esther, and I did also. We all later admitted that he appeared to have a demented look in his eyes. The very thought that Naomi was in such hands made us shudder. Again, the tempter came and filled us with anger, which we had to deal with.

From the beginning, we detected that Penn Glazier, Anderson's appointed attorney, was a shrewd lawyer who could play his part well. We did not like it.

The pathologist testified again. He showed Glazier a hard time. At one point he pretended he was hard of hearing when he did not want to answer certain questions that Glazier asked. He would evade any questions that he could. Then he would lick his lips and glance at Detective Henry out of the corner of his eyes. Henry's face showed no expression, but we felt sure that he was amused. We could see that it took effort on Glazier's part to keep his cool.

Detective Henry testified next. When Glazier asked him if any fingerprints were found on the knife, Anderson was shaking his head "no," with his long hair swinging from side to side. His attorney whispered something to Anderson and he whispered back. It was plain to see that Anderson knew that they had no fingerprints. Possibly his attorney had told him. It appeared as if Glazier deliberately wanted to prove Henry to be a liar in Anderson's presence.

Glazier then got permission from the judge (everything was whispered) to have the hearing closed to the public for the rest of

Henry's testimony and also for the testimony of Richard Sheetz. Henry told us on the way home that the first that he was aware of what was going on was when Glazier shoved a paper over to him, making the request. The judge then dismissed the hearing and put a gag order on the case, meaning those involved in the case were not to talk about it until the trial to avoid publicity.

We were all out in the hallway of the courthouse while Henry and Sheetz testified behind closed doors. It was confusing for us until we learned what was going on. They were playing the tape of Anderson's confession. It took about thirty minutes and we were then all allowed to go back in the courtroom. In about ten minutes we were dismissed.

As everyone was leaving the courtroom, Esther and I were two of the last ones in our row to leave since most of the people filed out before us. We noticed that two girls were hesitating to leave the room and kept looking at Anderson, but his back was turned. One of the officers in charge of the crowd approached them and wondered what they wanted. They said they would like to talk to Anderson. The officer replied flatly, "No conversations!" Anderson must have heard what was going on because as they were leading him out the side door, he looked back at them and said, "I'll call you later." We could not believe how brazen he was!

Before we left for home we were visiting out in the hall with the other Huyards. Rebecca and I noticed one lady who kept close to a couple who belonged to the Salvation Army. Her face was tear-stained and we felt we should talk with her. She told us that Anderson came from a broken home and she was his aunt. Anderson lived with her until he was fourteen. She did not offer more about his life from then on and we were careful in our conversation with her.

We asked if she had thought Anderson was capable of killing anyone. She instantly replied, "I don't believe he did it, and I never will!" This took us by surprise and we decided we had better not stir her up. She did express sorrow for us. She didn't believe he did it, yet she was very sympathetic with us. Her attitude was quite different from the Billers and it warmed our hearts toward her. We told her we could not be certain either who killed Naomi, but we know someone did. We told her that maybe these boys thought they could try anything with an Amish girl and could get away with it, thinking we would not cooperate with the law. We also told her that we abided by the law and we were going to let them deal with it. I guess we told her this, hoping she would tell Anderson.

Later in the summer, after Danny's trial, that couple from the Salvation Army came out to visit us. They told us that after Anderson's hearing, his aunt told them that she thought we were very nice girls. We were surprised to hear this because we had not talked with her very much, plus, she knew we did not agree with her.

The Billers were also at the hearing. They seemed almost happy. We soon detected that they were now sure that Danny would be excused and they seemed very ready to push everything on Anderson. We tried to avoid them because we did not agree with them. We asked Leona if they had ever seen Anderson before, or known him. She said she had known him because he was one of Danny's friends and that he lived at their house for a week in October. We were shocked to hear that they allowed such a person to live in their home.

Leona then asked Mary if she received Danny's letter. She had not. Leona told her she was getting one since Danny wanted to apologize. Later she was heard telling their minister's wife that Danny's lawyer advised Danny to write Mary a letter of apology, thinking it might help him out in some way. In our minds we had no doubt that if Mary would get a letter from him, it would have been composed by the lawyer himself. Things did not quite add up. Why would Leona think Danny should apologize when she thought he was innocent of any crime!? Mary never received a letter from him.

On the way home, Mary told Detective Henry that it really hurts her to see the Billers so happy, now that they can put the blame on the other guy. She was not prepared for Henry's reaction. He banged his fist on the steering wheel and said, "Danny Biller is a murderer!" He said Danny participated in everything except the stabbings and that Naomi would have died without the stab wounds. That only finished her up. She would certainly have died from the beatings and shock alone. He said he also noticed the Billers' attitude, but that they have no reason to be happy.

Hans approached Detective Henry at the courthouse and said he was hearing rumors that Danny could still get the electric chair and he wondered if that was true. Henry cooly answered, "Sure," and walked off.

When we asked Henry if he noticed how Anderson gave the thumbs up signal to his buddy, he said incredulously, "Did he do that? The dirty ___!" We were almost shocked at his language because it was so unlike his character, but we knew it was his outlet for the vehemence he felt inside.

At times, when we talked with Nettles or Henry, we would express sympathy for both boys with their wrecked lives. Mary expressed it as such a shame for their young lives to be wasted, to which Nettles deliberately expressed his view and said, "We feel it is a shame Naomi had to die in such a way." We detected that they wanted us to keep our spunk up until the trial was over.

We really wondered how they would be able to prove that Anderson was at the Biller house that evening, but we trusted the police entirely and prayed that justice would be done.

The whole thing was so exhausting. We would hear snatches of what Naomi might have suffered, but we certainly did not realize the extent of it. Dick Reeser, the district judge who lives in New Holland, remarked to his wife, who told me, "That girl must have suffered a lot!" I knew he must know what he was talking about because he had read all the court manuscripts and had been the judge for both hearings. I did cleaning for the Reesers so I knew Dick and I knew he wasn't one to talk unnecessarily about his cases. Naomi's suffering must have been bad for him to make such a remark—but I didn't want to believe it.

In the evenings, Mary would draw her shades down the whole way on the windows which faced the Biller home. That house looked foreboding, especially at night. Sometimes when I looked out at the house, at all the windows in the breezeway facing the road, going from the garage to the house, I imagined Naomi on her way to the basement, looking longingly toward our farm thinking, "Help seems so close, yet it's so far away." We will never know what she was thinking....

—— **Chapter 10** ——

Company, which came every Sunday and also during the week, was still a big help, as was the mail. I discovered for myself that when I went away to see my friends on Sundays, I felt so different than I did at home. I was much more relaxed and did not feel so afraid. That fear seemed to center the strongest at home, in the immediate area. Always, when Stevie and I would come out our road on our way home on a Sunday night, I would feel that familiar feeling of fear and dread return inside me.

One Sunday night, as we were approaching the Biller home, we noticed a light in the bathroom. A chill went through me. I glanced at Stevie and he glanced at me. We both just shook our heads but had nothing to say. It was still so hard to believe that something like this happened so close to home.

I feel sure now that it was with the help of a Higher Power that none of us ended up with mental problems that first year. A good friend of ours, who is a psychiatrist, said she knows of a superb psychiatrist in Lancaster who would be glad to talk with us. She said that any visits we want to make there would all be paid. Rebecca and Mother went twice and were glad they went.

On April 15, the whole front page of the morning paper was filled with an article regarding the story Danny told his cellmate one day in January about Anderson's involvement in the murder. The article was in poor taste and not meant for the public because it was actually an account of Danny's lies. The police were not happy to see it in print and had no idea how the reporters got their story. It was a very gross story of the murder.

On the following day another article was printed, stating that the cellmate had to be put in solitary confinement because of the article. The authorities did not want to risk a jail hassle with Anderson or any of his buddies. Meanwhile, Danny was having weird hang-ups in prison. Once he was found in his cell completely stripped of his clothing. Henry told us that Anderson and Biller were never released together in prison.

On April 27 another long article was printed stating that the Biller trial was scheduled to be in the Lancaster Courthouse sometime in May. It went on to say how the district attorneys are seeking first degree murder charges for both boys. A first degree murder charge automatically carries a penalty of either life imprisonment or the death penalty. The district attorneys wanted the death penalty for both boys.

In order for a murderer to be sentenced to death, the prosecution must prove that the aggravating circumstances outweigh the mitigating circumstances. Here, so far, the aggravating circumstances were murder by means of torture, murder committed while in furtherance of a felony (robbery or rape), and murder of a victim who was a witness to a felony committed by the defendants and was killed for the purpose of preventing her testimony against the felony.

The mitigating circumstances, so far, were the age, lack of maturity, or youth of the defendant. The police described both boys to us as sadists, which means enjoying to torture.

On May 4, a newspaper article stated that the Biller trial was postponed and the trial will be moved out of the county because of all the publicity. The defense attorney said Danny could not have a fair trial in Lancaster County. It would be hard to find a jury of twelve people in Lancaster County who knew nothing about the facts of the case.

The prosecuting attorneys and police wanted to have one trial, taking both boys together, but the defense attorneys would not allow it. It would have been easier for all the witnesses involved to just go to a trial one time instead of two, and would have been only half as expensive for the state. They would have gotten both boys to testify against each other, **if** they would have done it.

Detective Henry asked our neighbor, Amy Tressler, if she would be willing to testify at Danny's trial, describing how she felt about Danny that night that she had seen him in their home with a knife. She cried and said she could not get up there and face him. Henry coaxed her until she finally consented to do it, but when the time came, he was not allowed to use this evidence.

Sometime in May, Henry came out and said the trial would not be in May after all, but was scheduled to begin on June 13 and would be held at the courthouse in Easton, Pennsylvania, which was a 2-1/2-hour drive. Henry also told us that Danny may decide to plead guilty, even on the day before the trial, which would mean there would not be a trial in Easton, but a short one would be held in the presence of a judge in Lancaster.

Lots of people asked us about going along to the trial. We asked Henry if it would be wise to take our friends along. He hesitated to tell us but said he was sure it would make a good impression on the jury if the Amish would attend the trial. He did not want to say much because if the defense attorney would hear it, he would try to use that for a reason for a mistrial. The defense attorney would certainly not advise us to take our friends, but it is important that the jury sees that Naomi had friends who cared for her. Otherwise they might think she was just a single girl with no family or friends who cared if the murderers were locked up or not.

We learned that the trial could take a week or more, but we had no way of knowing. We encouraged people to go and tried to arrange that two van loads would go each day. The thought of the oncoming trial weighed heavily on our minds and bodies.

One Sunday forenoon we were all at home, singing together before company came. We thought we would ask Mary to come and join us because this was something she and Naomi often did with us on Sunday forenoons. One of us went over to tell Mary but returned saying, "Mary is sitting there, weeping." Being alone with grief is very lonesome, but every individual has to pour out sometime. We didn't have the spirit to sing anymore then either.

On Friday, June 10, an officer from the Ephrata barracks came out and brought subpoenas for Mary and Rebecca to appear at the trial as witnesses. Mom talked with him awhile. She asked him if we really **have** to go. He looked sharply at her and said, "You'll want to be there!" He told us that after they pick the jurors the first few days, the trial will begin.

The police from the Ephrata barracks remarked that it is high time the Amish people wake up and become aware of what goes on in the rest of the world outside their tight circle. They said this might be a learning experience for everyone to make us aware of the evil that is around us, and also to learn the system of the law.

We didn't encourage anyone to go the first day, which was on Monday, June 13, the day the jurors were being picked in Easton. We were not there, but our neighbors, the Tresslers, kept us informed of the proceedings. They were keeping tab of it via the news on the radio. In the evening they told us that nine jurors were picked. The papers were again filled with the news.

On Tuesday, June 14, around 5:00 in the morning, a load of us started for Easton. Andy Fisher went with us, which was a help to us. The murder trial for their daughter had also been held at that same courthouse because of all the publicity in Lancaster County.

The courthouse was an old one. The officials in charge were very kind and respectful. At 9:00 they began by picking jurors again which certainly was a learning experience to watch. We wished there would have been more Amish there to see how it's done. The judge, Michael Perezous, sat up in his pew on a large stuffed chair, wearing a dark robe. He was a shrewd man with dark glittering eyes that seemed to look clear through you. Henry told us we were lucky to have him because he does his job right.

Hardly anything took place without the judge noticing it. A lady in the audience sat in the back row, knitting. She was given the choice to leave the room or quit knitting. Nothing was allowed which might distract the jurors' attention.

Reese, the defense attorney, and Danny sat on the left side of the room, facing the judge and the witness stand. They sat a few arm lengths in front of us, with a three-foot-high partition dividing us.

There were rows of benches for the audience and could probably hold about 100 people. The district attorney and Detective Henry sat on the right side of the room. Richard Sheetz was more valuable as a witness now, after his interviews with Danny, so Joseph Madenspracher took his place as district attorney. He was also a very nice gentleman who took sharp notice of everything that was going on.

Danny Biller hardly looked like the same person who had been at his hearing. The attorney had him all cleaned up, wearing a suit and glasses. His clean-cut hairdo was the greatest contrast.

The attorneys had thirty men and women from which they could pick out twelve jurors (plus two spares). They brought each one in separately and questioned them. If the person answered to their liking, he was accepted as a juror. Danny also had the right to turn one down if he wished.

One of the first questions our attorney asked each person was whether they agreed that the death penalty was appropriate for certain first degree murder cases. If they did not agree to this, they were dismissed, because this was a first degree murder charge and they were seeking the death penalty.

If they did agree, they were asked more questions such as: what type of job they held, if they were married, or had children.

One of the first questions the defense attorney asked was whether they knew anything about the Amish and their beliefs. If they did, he was quick to ask them their attitude about the Amish. Very few of those thirty people knew anything about the Amish and those who knew anything showed a good attitude. The defense attorney dismissed them. After one was chosen, he or she was given strict orders not to talk to any of the witnesses or those involved. They were advised to not even say hello if they chanced to meet them in the halls or the street.

It was amazing to us that we didn't have to be farther away from home than Easton and find very few people who knew anything about the Amish. The citizens in Easton stared at us. I wished with my whole heart that we Amish people would all live up to what these strangers expected of us.

By 10:00 all fourteen jurors were chosen. They were all seated on chairs at a separate area of the courtroom, along the side. Judge Perezous then gave a lengthy lecture concerning the law. The courtroom was very quiet despite the fact that there were around fifty spectators in the room. The Billers and their minister were also there.

The judge informed the jurors that they were allowed to go home overnight, but they weren't allowed to read the paper or watch TV or mention any facts of the case to any other human being—or even to each other. Only when they were ready to deliberate were they allowed to talk to each other.

The jury consisted of eight men and four women who were anything from housewives, factory workers, to businessmen. They sat with rapt attention. The judge informed them that **they** will be the sole judge of the verdict of this case, whether it was first, second, or third degree murder, or voluntary manslaughter. He told them that he was only there to make sure everything proceeds according to the law.

He told them that in order to convict a defendant of third degree or less, it has to be proven that the victim was dead and that the murderer was killing out of passion or self-defense. For a second degree charge, the victim was dead and was killed following a felony (rape or robbery). For a first degree charge it also has to be proven that the victim was dead and was killed following a felony which was also pre-meditated. He explained that pre-meditated could be as simple as the defendant holding his weapon (which caused the death) and thinking, "Will I kill or will I not?"

He also explained that an accomplice for any type of murder was charged the same as the actual murderer. If he didn't even participate, but just watched, he was still as guilty as the murderer because he didn't aid the victim or go for help.

The seriousness of their job was thoroughly impressed upon them before the trial began when they were asked by the judge, "Do you believe that for your decision this week, be it right or wrong, that you will be responsible for—before the almighty God—on that last great day?" They all rose with their right hand raised and replied in unison, "I do." A solemn stillness filled the room. The court was then dismissed for a break. All the spectators were to remain seated until the jurors filed out of the room and disappeared.

One thing we noticed that was different from Lancaster was that not one club or gun was in sight on any of the officers. But we knew they were available, for once, outside the courtroom, we saw Detective Henry put his hand in his pocket and accidentally raise the edge of his tuxedo. We spied a small handgun hanging on his belt. We were always sort of awestruck by Henry. He seemed like such a gentle person.

At noon the trial began. The spectators filed in first, then the attorneys and Danny, and last of all the jury filed in. The judge walked in the side door and stepped up to his seat. Madenspracher opened up by relating the story of the case to the jurors.

We learned more details, which made us feel sick. He said that after Naomi stepped in on the boys, while they were stealing meat, and had talked to them, Danny remarked to Anderson, "Let's have some fun." As

67

they approached her, she stepped back, tripped, and fell. They attacked her and tied her hands and feet. Anderson picked up her glasses and threw them behind the freezer, which explained how that frame got there. They dragged her downstairs with her begging for release. Danny's story was that Anderson told him to get two pairs of gloves and his tackle box, which they took along down to the basement. They ripped off her clothing, and untied her hands and feet to take off the rest of her clothing. They started tormenting her in ways which I will not describe in detail. Finally, she was beaten, strangled, and stabbed.

After Madenspracher was finished talking, Reese got up and also made a speech. His speech was longer and he tried to convince the jury not to judge too hastily and tried, whenever he could, to point out where Madenspracher might be wrong, or even where he might have incorrectly worded his statements.

My sister Rebecca was then called upon to testify. The procedure of questions was practically the same as it had been at the hearing. Reese didn't ask her this time why she telephoned the Biller home instead of going over in person before the search began. He didn't want her to say she was afraid to go over in the presence of a jury. This would have shown Danny's former character to the jury. Anything that he said or did prior to this crime had to be completely silent, by law. Yet the defense council had the right to bring to light any of the criminal's good points or deeds prior to the happening. The terrible-looking hairstyle of these criminals, how they looked at the time of the crime was not known, yet the defense had the right to clean them up and make them appear as perfect gentlemen. The jury had no way of knowing their lifestyle prior, or at the time of the happening. In my mind, I wondered if the jurors suspected any of Danny's prior lifestyle.

Mary was next called upon to testify. She remained very calm and composed, although it was a terrible mental strain for her. Her face expressed a very sad, weary expression. She had to identify Naomi's broken lenses, dental plate, and her clothing, plus several pieces of underwear. After she was done, the court was dismissed for the day. The Billers weren't asked to testify. Nettles and Henry told us it is risky business to get parents of a defendant to testify because sometimes they change their story on the witness stand and are not to be trusted.

The police and investigators had reservations made for themselves at a motel in Easton for that week, but we came home overnight. As soon as we stepped outside the courtroom, reporters were there and wanted to talk to us. Photographers were also there, taking a lot of pictures. This went on all week. One photographer kept running ahead of us as we walked up the sidewalk and took our picture. As we neared him, he backed up to get another one. While he was doing this, he backed into a pillar and it did amuse us. He then said, "Sorry, it's my job," waved at us, and went on his way.

When we arrived home, we had company who wanted to hear about our day. David and Esther stayed at our house overnight. Rebecca stayed in Easton so David and Esther slept in her room which adjoins mine, with a door between our rooms. Sleeping was impossible for me that night because I was afraid. The others didn't sleep well either. It was a strange feeling to feel that way. I felt as if an iron hand gripped at my chest and twisted it. Finally, toward morning, I started sobbing. David and Esther were not asleep either and Esther then came to my room and stayed with me. We got up at 4:00 and I had not slept at all.

At 5:00 on Wednesday morning, we started for Easton again. This was the roughest day. The courtroom was packed with approximately sixty Amish people, plus Hans and Leona Biller and their minister, and most of our neighbors.

In the morning, before the court was in session, Nettles and Henry called Mom and Mary aside and asked about our setup with the freezer in the Biller garage. They said the Billers approached them yesterday and implied that Mary lied on the witness stand, saying they didn't know that Mary and Naomi used the freezer. We didn't realize they didn't know this, for there was never any question about it. We and the aunts shared our things. The police and we agreed—What difference did all this make in the murder, and why mention it?

Trooper Nettles testified first. His story was practically what it had been at the hearing. Madenspracher then brought out some enlarged photographs. Reese objected that they be used as evidence so both attorneys and the judge debated about it in a side room. Reese, time and again, objected to different uses of evidence that Madenspracher wanted to use. Sometimes it was granted to him by the judge and sometimes it wasn't. Several of the photos were allowed to be used, but not the ones with the whole body of the victim exactly as she was found. We could not see the photos from where we sat. Several of them were photos of the house, the basement, and the freezer. There was one of the body, partially covered, and this was passed along to the jurors. Detective Henry told us later that he was really surprised that the judge did not object to this. He also said there was a lot more evidence that they had wanted to use, but it was objected by Reese and turned down by the judge.

Richard Sheetz testified next. Most of his testimony was statements given to him by Danny at an inverview on March 7. There were several dozen pages of statements, but Reese objected to Sheetz reading them. Instead, he had to relate these statements in detail by memory. In these statements, Danny had finally admitted going along to the basement and helping to rip off Naomi's clothing and beating her when she wouldn't cooperate with them in their sexual desires. Danny said she prayed. Then Anderson asked Danny for his knife. Danny gave it to him and he started stabbing her. It never came to light when or who used the cord to strangle her. Danny also said she had no underwear on, which was already proven a lie, for Mary had identified her underwear on the witness stand the day before.

Henry then testified again how Danny's first story had been that he was not at home on Saturday evening but was at four different places looking for jobs. These four clerks again testified that he had not been there at all. A neighbor, Rev. Good, also testified that he was searching with Danny that night in the fields and when he asked Danny whether Naomi could be in the basement of the house, Danny said she couldn't be. Henry also testified how Danny gave him another story in March. It was practically the same as his story to Sheetz had been. We knew, although it wasn't brought out in court, that the day he had finally admitted these statements to Sheetz and Henry was the day they had tested him with a lie detector test and Henry dared him to tell another lie.

While Sheetz was testifying, Leona Biller turned around in her seat and said to our neighbors, "They're all lies!" Nobody really answered her.

None of us felt like eating at our lunch break. Mary went to the restroom and wept like a child and we wept with her. My eyes were getting dim from loss of sleep and the strain of shedding tears. I finally could not see the judge clearly anymore. I felt sick, and I wasn't the only one. In the afternoon it again was very quiet in the courtroom.

Danny Biller took the witness stand, by his own request. Defendants have the right to choose whether they want to testify on their own behalf or not. When Danny got up on the witness stand, Hans and Leona Biller both burst into loud crying.

Detective Henry turned around in his seat to see what was going on. It was the first time he did this and he had a look of disapproval on his face. He later told us that it's a common thing for defense attorneys to stage members of the defendant's family to cry during certain periods at their trial so that the jurors will take pity on the defendant. Henry told us of cases where it actually swung the jury to acquit the defendant. Whether this was the reason for their outburst, we do not know. Two of the security officers led them out of the courtroom and they didn't hear Danny's testimony on the witness stand. We wished they would have heard it because then they might have been more willing to look at the facts of the case. They should have heard Danny get tangled in his own lies. But lies seemed like a minor thing at this point, yet how serious lying is!

As long as Reese was questioning Danny on the witness stand, he didn't appear too bad. Reese was quick to point out to the jury that Danny was an adopted child and would have liked to give the appearance of a rough home life.

Over the process of questioning, Danny came out with still another different story. This time he declared Anderson attacked her by himself in the garage and dragged her to the kitchen and asked Danny to go along to the basement. Partway down the stairway Anderson kicked Naomi in the back and sent her sprawling down the stairs. The only thing he admitted to doing was helping to rip off her clothing and watching Anderson torture her. He claimed he went upstairs then and didn't watch the murder. I don't think anyone in the room believed his story at all.

When Madenspracher began questioning him, it was actually pathetic. He had him so tangled up in his own lies at times that he didn't know what to say anymore. When Danny was asked whether Naomi spoke to them, he said she was praying and kept repeating, "Please don't hurt me." Then Anderson would say, "Shut up ___." I will not repeat the language. This we did believe because it was exactly the language that was used by Manson in the book *Helter Skelter*.

It was obvious, for anyone who had been following all prior testimony, to see that the story given to Sheetz and Henry by Danny on March 7 was the only story that held some truth and made sense. Danny didn't appear so sure of himself anymore. Following Danny's testimony, the court was dismissed for the day. We again started for home around 5:00. Rebecca and one of her friends stayed in Easton at a motel for the night.

We had quite a bit of work to do at home in the evenings. It was in the midst of our strawberry season. Jean Tressler brought our supper down and helped us pick and freeze the berries until we were done, which was pretty late. It was a long, hard day—probably the worst day we ever lived through. To try and sleep much this night was out of the question. One of my friends came home overnight with me, for which I was very glad. Without the support of true friends, I don't know how we would have all survived and remained sane. I'm sure they didn't realize how much it meant to us.

71

—— Chapter 11 ——

On Thursday morning, June 16, all of us again started out for Easton. The courtroom was again packed with people, mostly Amish. Before the court was open, Esther and I talked a few minutes with Detective Henry in the cafeteria. We asked him how he slept last night. He said he didn't sleep well because he had an upset stomach. Yes, they're human, too.

We learned that the proceedings for today would be the closing argument of the two attorneys. The prosecution had the final speech in this. The court again started at 9:00. I thought all twelve jurors actually looked weary. The defense attorney stood up in front of the jurors and began talking. He paced the floor and it was obvious that he said anything in his power to try and convince the jury that Danny was not guilty of any wrong. His final words to the jury were asking them to acquit Danny of all charges. We certainly hoped the jury would have more common sense than that.

The prosecuting attorney then spoke for about a half hour. He spoke calmly and sensibly, but you could detect a force behind his speech. He asked the jury to return with a verdict of first degree murder. The judge then gave another speech informing the jury of the law concerning deliberations. The court was dismissed at noon.

The jury went into a separate room in the courthouse with no one else present. If they had any questions concerning the law, they were allowed to send a messenger to the judge for their answers. But the decision was solely theirs. We decided we would wait around the courthouse until 5:00, hoping the jury would reach a decision before we went home. I'm sure many prayers went up to God on behalf of the jury to help them reach a "just" decision.

While we were waiting, a group of us met the Billers and their minister in the hallway. It seemed as if they were ready to lash out at anyone at this point. More words were said in those fifteen minutes than were necessary. We were accused of not being forgiving because we didn't agree with them that Danny should be allowed another chance at freedom.

We told the Billers that we felt Danny did not deserve freedom because he was a menace to society. Even if a child does wrong you can forgive him, but he must be punished (as a warning to others, if nothing else). They told us that boys like Danny start out with tobacco, then drugs, then worse things. They pointed their finger at us and said, "Who raises this tobacco but **you** people!" We were appalled by their attitude and had no idea that they

73

were harboring all these ill feelings.

What they said about raising tobacco was very disturbing because in knowing that it was offensive to the Billers, how many others are we offending? What kind of a Christian "Light" are we? When thinking of how opposed our forefathers (especially Jacob Amman) were to any form of using or raising tobacco, and the stand that they took against it, it was shocking to have such a decline in our faith pointed out. It made me feel very sad. But, despite facing those facts, does that excuse a murder?

It was harder to forgive Danny than Anderson because he knew Naomi while Anderson did not. But a Christian must forgive, yes, even the worst murderers. My thoughts were of how Jesus prayed for those who crucified Him: "Father, forgive them for they know not what they do." I do believe Naomi would say it was worth it if those boys would come to see the Light. My heart ached for them.

To be accused of not being forgiving after such an ordeal and having to deal with those feelings was as hard for us as the murder itself. Pages could be written on our feelings in that area, but would it help anything? We have to control our own feelings, and others wouldn't understand them anyway. It didn't seem fair, but life has never been fair for Christians. Life goes on.... Many thoughts fill our minds. Some are good and some are not so good. We must turn some away and be shepherd and bishop of our souls. If we carried a grudge or hated Danny or his parents, or anyone else, we would be no better than a murderer ourselves.

Hans Biller later came and apologized for what he said and it meant a great deal to us. I pitied him with my whole heart. Leona said, "I still don't think Danny did any wrong to Naomi, but it was wrong of him not to go for help for her."

While we were waiting in the courthouse, two men approached me as I was standing by myself and asked me several questions about this case. They said they were guards at the Easton Prison and asked if we would like to tour the prison. I was very hesitant and they noticed that I mistrusted them. They shrugged their shoulders and grinned at each other. Then the one guard got out his wallet and showed me his card, proving his occupation. We walked over to the rest of our group and asked them if they would like a tour. No one was really enthused, but the guards finally persuaded us.

Not more than six of us were allowed in one group for the tour. We walked out around the building and entered. At the doorway was a small room where a man sat with earphones on, facing a large computer. He didn't as much as glance our way. The guards explained that he operates every door in the prison, including each cell door, by that computer. As we approached the door leading directly into the prison, the guard pressed a button and said a few numbers; then the door slowly opened. It closed again behind us with a clang, which made me shudder. All the doors, including the cell doors, were cage-like, metal doors. We happened to arrive in prison while the prisoners had recess. An hour each day all the prisoners, except the real bad ones, are allowed to be together for a break. It actually looked like a human zoo. The guards walked through the crowd fearlessly. The rest of us huddled together. We walked so close by the prisoners that we could have touched them. Some of them had blank expressions on their faces, others gave us curious stares, while others yelled after us. One came charging after us with his arms spread apart as if to grab one of us. The guard just gave him a gentle shove.

We learned that the guards carry no keys or weapons for self-defense, but they all practice karate. They told us there are over 200 prisoners in their prison which is overcrowded. They took us through a narrow passage leading to the kitchen. Then we passed a line of prisoners who were waiting their turn for a shower. They stared after us. Last of all, the guards showed us the cages where the hardened criminals were. They hardly appeared human to me by the expressions on their faces. There should be a better way for human beings, yet they are there by their own choice. I breathed a sigh of relief after we left the prison.

We waited for another hour, hoping that the jurors would find a verdict. After 5:00 they still had not returned, so we started for home. Our evening at home was a long one, filled with tense waiting. The days and nights were warm and humid, draining our strength. We went to bed late and still no one called. Detective Henry had Tresslers' phone number and he had said he would call as soon as the verdict came back.

On Friday morning, June 17, we were working outside in the garden when our neighbor, Jimmy Tressler, came peddling down on his bicycle. Soon after 9:00, Henry had called the Tresslers, informing them that the verdict was first degree murder. (He also called David's.) A great weight was lifted from our beings.

The jurors had deliberated until 9:00 p.m. on Thursday evening and could not agree on a decision. They were advised to go home, to think and pray about the verdict. On Friday morning it took only ten minutes to agree.

The Billers had started for Easton on Friday morning, but weren't there in time to hear the verdict announced. The jurors then had to decide the punishment. The defense attorney presented character witnesses on Danny's behalf. In other words, they were fighting for Danny's life.

Henry promised he would call again on the final verdict. Now we again felt a suspense, but the suspense consisted mostly of a feeling of heaviness. We resigned ourselves to the fact that his life depended solely on the letter of the law. Henry had told us earlier that we have no say in the matter concerning his punishment. I asked Mary how she would feel if Danny's punishment would be death. She hesitated before answering. Then she said, "We had nothing to say to it when the killing occurred, and we have nothing to say to the punishment, either."

Whenever we were confronted by reporters concerning our views on the punishment, our answer was, "He placed himself in the hands of the law and now he's in the law's hands." (Rebecca or Dad always did the talking to the reporters.) We prayed earnestly for God's will. A Christian policeman suggested that we read and study Romans 13, which we did and found it very helpful:

"1) Let every soul be subject unto the higher powers. For there is no power but of God: the powers that be are ordained of God.

"2) Therefore, whosoever resisteth the power, resisteth the ordinance of God: and they that resist shall receive to themselves damnation.

"3) For rulers are not a terror to good works, but to the evil. Wilt thou then not be afraid of the power? Do that which is good, and thou shalt have praise of the same.

"4) For he is a minister of God to thee for good. But if thou do that which is evil, be afraid; for he beareth not the sword in vain: for he is the minister of God, a revenger to execute wrath upon him that doeth evil.

"5) Wherefore ye must needs be subject, not only for wrath, but also for conscience sake."

We knew that if we, personally, would take the law in our own hands and would punish the evil doers out of revenge, we'd be as bad as any murderer. But it was our belief that the law has the right to punish them as they see fit. It is not like some people might picture it—that we could step up to Danny at his trial and tell him we forgive him, etc.

Someone specifically made it a point to ask us our opinion on the death penalty, and we gave them the same answer as we did the reporters. They told us we are taking the cowardly way out, and went on to tell us a story they had heard or read somewhere of a couple whose daughter had been killed; the parents walked up to the defendant at his trial, laid their hands on his shoulder, and told him they forgive him. In the end he was converted. We made no comments to this couple. It made a nice story, but it is very unrealistic. It was obvious that this couple was never in a courtroom or they would know such a thing wasn't possible. There is a three-foot-high wooden wall between the spectators' benches and the opening of the place where the defendant and his attorney sit. If we would have tried to cross over there, we would have been taken out of the court-room very quickly. We have to be forgiving, but evil doers must be dealt with also. "Because sentence against an evil work is not executed speedily, therefore the heart of the sons of men is fully set in them to do evil" (Ecc. 8:11).

At approximately 10:30, Henry called out to Tresslers again and announced that the verdict was life imprisonment, with parole, as usual. It was a relief to us that his life had been spared, but it was a disappointment to the prosecutors. Their theory was, if this kind of crime does not deserve the death penalty, what ever will?" And why does Pennsylvania carry the death penalty law if it is not being used? Their theory made sense, but we were afraid to state our opinion either way.

The Billers were devastated by the verdict and asked the reporters how they think those jurors would feel if it was **their** son who received such a punishment. Most of the jurors' comments to the reporters were that it was the hardest job they ever had. Quite a few reporters came out to talk to us. Mary made no comments and Dad voiced his comments very carefully, for fear of hurting the Billers. Attorney Reese remarked that it was the messiest case he ever handled, and he hopes he will never undertake one like it again. (They do have a choice.)

Detective Henry later told us that the reason it took the jurors such a long time to deliberate was because they had a unanimous vote for first degree murder charge in a short time, except for one juror, and the reason he did not give up easily was because he had a son of his own with a jail record. For us to hear this, it seemed like the blind leading the blind. Henry said it was a mistake that that wasn't checked out properly while choosing jurors.

Following the trial, we again received an avalanche of company, which we appreciated. We cooked many, many meals for company. Our crop of potatoes was gone long before the winter was over.

In August, there was a closed hearing with the state trooper from Florida. Anderson's attorney was trying his best to figure out the best way out for Anderson. After hearing Anderson's confession on tape at his hearings, Glazier knew that those tapes were the only full proof of Anderson's part in the murder, so he sent in appeals to the United States Supreme Court, asking that the tapes not be used at Anderson's trial, along with a list of other appeals. He handed a complaint in that Anderson was threatened and badgered in Florida until he confessed and he wanted that to be used on Anderson's behalf at his trial. Anderson was sorry he talked so much after hearing his confessions on tape, and now he refused to talk at interviews, by the advice of his attorney, of course. But it was too late; the confessions were made. His appeals were all turned down except one, which was that he was granted a change of venue (trial moved out of county). His trial was then scheduled for Schuylkill County, which was a three-hour drive also.

Meanwhile, many van loads of Amish were again arranging to attend the trial. We wondered how the courtroom would hold them all.

Detective Henry told us there is no doubt that a jury will be rough on Anderson up in Schuylkill County, because there are many coal miners up there and they are rough people. Schuylkill County is also heavily populated with Catholics and the Catholics are very protective of their nuns. In their eyes, Naomi would have been a nun, being single and dedicating her life to others. Penn Glazier also thought of this as we later learned that he had gone up and checked out that part of the county. He certainly exerted himself to win this case. What a way to make a living....

Anderson's trial was scheduled to begin on October 17. We had arrangements all made for that week. Rebecca and Mary had their subpoenas, along with many others, to appear as witnesses at the trial the following Monday.

On Thursday evening, October 13, an officer came to our door bearing a message from Detective Henry, saying Mary and Rebecca were to appear at the Lancaster Courthouse on Friday morning. Anderson had pleaded guilty. This was a confusion to us for we had no idea if anyone else was supposed to go along, or even if they may, or what the court procedures would be. No one seemed to know. We called Mose and he didn't know. Finally, I called our district justice, for whom I was working. He said the Court is open to the public, so we decided we won't tell this to others outside of our immediate family because it was too short notice.

Mom, David, Esther, Mary, Rebecca, and I decided to go. Around 8:00 that evening Mose came out and said our attorney, John Keneff, nearly panicked when he learned that the Amish were not intending to attend the trial.

Mose had called Rod Hartman, our town cop, about information on whether the Court is open to the public. Rod talked with John Keneff, which is how he got wind of it.

At 9:00 that evening we went to the phone and called a few people from our church district, etc., who said they would get people together. On Friday morning at 8:30 we arrived at the courthouse. We could see by the expression on Keneff's face that it was a relief to him to see all the Amish in attendance, although it was hidden from anyone who wasn't closely observing. Rod Hartman, the town cop, also came in with a few of his neighbors. He wanted to be sure that some (just anyone) Amish were there.

As we were sitting there and everything was very quiet, Judge Eckman took his place and Detective Henry also walked in with Penn Glazier and another guy with a suit on. Esther and I were trying to figure out who the third gentleman was. Suddenly Esther said, "That has to be Anderson!" I didn't agree with her because there was no likeness to him and the evil-looking guy who had walked in during his hearing. However, as the Court took session, we all realized it was Anderson. We didn't recognize him at all. He had a neat haircut, a suit on, seemed very respectful, and was carrying a Bible. My first thoughts were, "My, such a shame for a boy who could have been so nice."

Henry, Glazier, and Anderson stood before Judge Eckman while he read the "rights" to Anderson. Eckman always asked him, "Do you understand?" to which he answered, "Yes, your honor." Actually, by his manner, etc., he won sympathy from some others who were present.

By this time we were up to the tricks of the defense and defendants, and also, we had seen his actions at the hearing, whereas the others had not. (At his hearing, he wasn't worried; he wasn't trying to impress a judge then.) It's different at a trial, but it would have been useless to try and explain this to anyone. Also, we knew we dare not voice our feelings on this for fear of others blaming us for being prejudiced. Again—only those in similar circumstances would ever understand this, unless they really tried.

Anderson was again given his choice of whether he still wished to change his mind and have a trial in the presence of a jury, but he persisted in wanting his trial before Judge Eckman. After a lunch break, the trial commenced. John Keneff started out by presenting the case, but quite a few details were omitted, which was because of the plea bargain. Mary was the first one called to the witness stand. She seemed nervous. Observing Anderson, one could tell he was watching every move Mary made. While she was testifying, he kept watching her. I really wondered what his thoughts were.

After the Court was dismissed, we were all standing out in the hallway visiting for a few minutes. One of our friends, Naomi Stoltzfus, found Anderson's aunt (the one with whom he lived) in the restroom, crying her heart out. Naomi put her arm around her and sympathized with her. The aunt said, "This must be such a loss for you people." She now believed that Anderson was involved, but she said she could not understand why he ever did such a thing. We figured this must be due to the fact that she had lost track of his lifestyle after his fourteenth year. We felt genuinely sorry for her. Here was a lady who did not pretend to go to church, yet she told us she was so sorry about this. She had no self-righteous attitude about her.

The trial was scheduled to continue on the following Tuesday, October 18.

Our hearts were heavy and exhausted....

On Tuesday the courtroom was packed with people. Anderson was again carrying a Bible. Surely Glazier knew this wouldn't impress Judge

Eckman. I suppose they were trying to impress the Amish people. Today those who testified were Trooper Nettles, Henry, Sheetz, the pathologist, Anderson's sister and aunt, and finally, a psychiatrist whom Glazier had chosen.

Henry, Nettles, and the pathologist's testimony were much the same as at Danny's trial, except in less words. Sheetz then ran the tapes of Anderson's confession. This was very, very hard for us to take. At one point in the tape, Anderson was asked why he stabbed her. He hesitated, then said, "She was starting to open her eyes, and tried so hard to say something. Then she tried to scream. I panicked and started to stab her...." Yes, we had a very clear picture of it all...but it was not clear to us who used the rope, etc. That part was never explained and it is still all left to our imagination.

After hearing those tapes, one knew Anderson had no choice but to plead guilty. Following this testimony, the Court was dismissed while Judge Eckman made his decision on which degree of murder to charge him. It took him approximately twenty minutes to deliberate. We were all very tense until he read the verdict as first degree murder. Now he had to decide on the matter of life or death as his punishment.

Character witnesses were brought forth, which were his aunt again, sister, and the psychiatrist. When the aunt testified, one could detect she was fighting for his life. She explained how Anderson had had a rough childhood and how she raised him from about seven years of age until fourteen. She explained how he was such an obedient boy, never talked back to her, never fought, and never disobeyed. It made a pitiful story, but we doubted all those "never dids."

At the end of all that, can our abused children who grow up and exercise violence on others as an outlet for their emotions be excused? What about the average citizen and his safety? It is a hard, hard situation and it is something that America has to deal with. But how? I am still convinced that all adults have choices of doing good or evil. God will not force us either way. If an individual chooses to do evil, someone has to be the victim—and God allows the happening, although I believe He chooses the victim....

In the aunt's testimony, no mention was made concerning Anderson's life from fourteen on, when he wasn't living with his aunt anymore. And why did he leave in the first place? The defense naturally didn't ask, and Keneff knew it would be useless to bring that up. If there had been anything bad, it would not have been held against him anyway.

Anderson's sister's testimony was much the same—a picture of a sad child- hood. We believe that the questions and answers between her and Glazier were all staged, although probably it was all quite true. His family originated in Virginia and one could easily tell it by a definite southern accent. He also kept watching his sister on the witness stand and I again wondered what his thoughts might be.

The psychiatrist then testified. Glazier had arranged for Anderson to see a psychiatrist following the murder. The psychiatrist testified that Anderson's I.Q. was below average and that he seemed mixed up. Who wouldn't be mixed up after murdering someone? He said Anderson was a follower and not a leader. Yet at Danny's trial it was testified that Danny was also a follower. Who was the leader then? The devil must have been.

The judge then asked the psychiatrist if he thought Anderson would repeat such a deed if he had a chance. The psychiatrist hesitated to say, but he said he could not be certain. He might participate in such a deed again if he had an accomplice and they had a good chance, but he thought it highly unlikely.

After his testimony, there was a half-hour break in which everyone remained seated, although the reason for it was unexplained. Henry told us on our way home that during that half hour he was trying to persuade Danny Biller to testify against Anderson, but he was not to be persuaded. It would have made things very bad for Anderson if Danny would have testified. In all this silent waiting, Anderson was sitting there, actually sweating. Finally, Glazier walked over to the judge and asked if Anderson could have a break. He was led back and out a side door.

The courtroom was heavily guarded at all sides with officers who had pistols and clubs hanging from their belts. To a casual observer, or one not deeply involved, it seemed unnecessary. But to those who knew the ways of Charles Manson and that Anderson was a Manson fan, it all made good sense. One didn't know what to expect from such a kind, but not a word of the Manson story was mentioned at the trial. This was also a part of his plea bargain, because Henry had said that would have all come out at his trial in Schuylkill County.

Finally the closing arguments began. Glazier talked for approximately an hour. He was a smooth talker and he had his facts all ready. He referred to previous cases and mentioned how others' lives were spared. While he was talking, Keneff was paging through his law book and occasionally glanced at Glazier respectfully. Time and again he would run his hand through his thick, wavy black hair while his face reflected a thoughtful expression. I wondered how one head could contain so much pressure and knowledge and remain sane.

In Glazier's final speech, he also tried to imply that no rape was involved with Anderson, only with Danny. If he could prove that no felony was involved before the murder, he could not be found guilty of first degree murder. He talked on and on, and leafed through dozens of his pages of literature. Before he finally took his seat, he looked at the judge and sort of pleadingly remarked, "I will never get used to the idea that the prosecuting side remains to have the last word." Judge Eckman remarked dryly, "You have done very well."

Keneff then got up for his final speech. He said a lot with a few words. He contradicted Glazier several times. He had a sneaky way of bringing out his point. He made it quite clear that rape was involved. He proved it by asking the court, "Why did Anderson admit that **they** tied her legs so she couldn't get away, but **they** tied the rope loosely for another purpose?"

He spoke approximately fifteen minutes before taking his seat. The Court was then dismissed while the judge went out to deliberate. He, alone, had the decision to make on the punishment. But he had to take all the evidence together and then go by the law to decide whether the mitigating circumstances outweigh the aggravating, or vice-versa.

In the hallway, Henry was sitting and reading the newspaper, looking neither right nor left. He did not invite conversation with anyone and his face had an expression which was hard to figure out. Most of us family members present didn't feel like talking at all, or even thinking. Many silent prayers went up to God. I felt sick.

The deliberation took approximately two and one-half hours. Finally, we were called in again. I waited until last to go in the door and I hesitated to enter because I wasn't sure I could handle the tension of waiting to hear the verdict sitting down. The sheriff by the door persuaded me to go in.

After everyone was seated, the courtroom was very, very quiet. The judge then read the verdict, which was life imprisonment (with parole— something the average citizen doesn't know). He decided that the mitigating circumstances outweighed the aggravating, according to the testimony given. He looked directly at Anderson and said, "The Court is showing more mercy to you than you showed to your victim." He and his attorney were then told on which date to appear in court for the formal sentencing. They were asked if they would appeal the sentencing and they both agreed they would not.

Finally, everything was over and we were dismissed. Some of our friends and also some outside my direct family lingered to speak with Anderson's family. Anderson's own father was at the trial. We were so ready to leave and did not feel like expressing ourselves to anyone.

The news reporters stopped us and talked with Mom and Dad. As we rounded the bend toward the elevators, I happened to glance back and noticed Penn Glazier looking our way. He smiled and waved. I hesitated and stared at him for an instant. Part of me rebelled to wave back. It took all my inner strength to raise my hand and wave. He looked too happy and it filled me with a dislike for him, but I felt better after returning his wave. This all took place in an instant, but a hundred thoughts can pass through one's mind at such a time.

On the way home we discussed the day's events. Detective Henry wondered if we noticed how Anderson was trying to outstare him while he was on the witness stand. We had not noticed. Henry said he continued to stare back at Anderson until he finally dropped his eyes. This was another idea that he got from Manson. Manson used to outstare the witnesses on the witness stand to try to confuse and scare them so that they couldn't testify properly. Manson had a devilish stare, and Anderson tried the same thing, but it didn't scare or confuse Henry. Anderson wasn't as bold and strong as he pretended to be. (And this was the same Anderson who had deceived some others into thinking that he was sorry at his trial.)

The police and prosecuting attorneys were disappointed that Anderson did not get the death penalty. They said that future murder cases would depend on this one. The defense council will defend their criminals by comparing this case to theirs. If this type of murder doesn't deserve the worst penalty, whatever will? But we were glad that the penalty wasn't death.

We cannot help but feel that someday there will be a fair trial before a just Judge, where there will be no plea bargaining and there will be no defense council. All the mists will be rolled away and we will understand everything....

Over on the Other Shore

Let me go where saints are going
To the mansions of the blest;
Let me go where my Redeemer
Has prepared His people rest.
I would gain the realms of brightness
Where they dwell forevermore;
I would join the friends that wait me
Over on the other shore.

Let me go where none are weary,
Where is raised no wail of woe;
Let me go and bathe my spirit
In the raptures angels know.
Let me go for bliss eternal
Lures my soul away, away,
And the victor's song triumphant
Thrills my heart—I cannot stay!

Let me go, why should I tarry?
What has earth to bind me here?
What but cares and toils and sorrows
What but death and pain and fear?
Let me go for hopes most cherished
Blasted 'round me often lie;
Oh, I've gathered brightest flowers
But to see them fade and die.

—one of Naomi Huyard's favorite hymns

—— Chapter 12 ——

After we were home, Mary's long-time teacher friend, Lydia Byler, came. She was a godsend. She was always a sturdy, dependable post and she again proved her true friendship. She wanted to hear all the details of our day.

Mary talked more than she did in a long time and it was very good for her to get the day's happenings out of her system. Before the evening was over, more company came, which were some single friends, and our talk continued.

They didn't approve of Mary, or us, talking about the day's happenings. One of them said, "Well, that is all over now; maybe it's time to talk about something else." They were the worst kind of visitors that Mary could have had at a time like this. We didn't answer her, but our thoughts all corresponded (even Lydia's). This company failed to realize, or try to imagine, that no one comes home from such a day in court and dismisses the whole matter. The best recovery for us, after such a day, was always to discuss everything and get it out of our system.

After the other company left, we continued our discussion. Lydia Byler stayed overnight and she and Mary talked long into the night. Her type of company was very helpful at such a time, but that other kind only hurt us, although we were very careful not to state our feelings. Very few people can understand such a situation.

A body goes through stages after such an ordeal. Sometimes you're so sick of hearing or thinking about it that you want to shut it completely out of your mind and pretend it didn't happen. Other times, when loneliness presses, it must come out again. Even now, after two years, the body still goes through these stages—fighting off fear, mixed emotions, forgiveness, and loneliness.

Most of the time it is easier to let the world go by and say nothing about it, because you get the feeling that no one would understand. For a long time after the trials, I couldn't talk about it. We received more mail again over this court trial. We received over 2,000 cards and letters among us.

We had heard rumors that the Billers would be moving out of the neighborhood, but we didn't know where or when. One Saturday in December we saw a moving van by the Billers. Mom made a pie and a pot of coffee and she and Dad took it over. Their motive in doing this was not for attention, but to help heal wounds. They discovered that the Billers were moving in with their daughter some distance away. Some of the Billers' church friends were there to help them move. Before they left,

Mom told Leona that we will always pray for Danny's soul, but we cannot pray for his release and we hope he will make things right with God for any part he played. Leona did not respond to this.

For some time I had troubled thoughts, wondering about Naomi's salvation. I thought of the many good deeds she had done in her life and yet, I knew she also had faults. Was she ready to die so suddenly?

I kept weighing this in my mind. If it depended on her good works to gain salvation, where does Jesus come in? If it depended on her good works, it would be like trying to gain heaven through our own righteousness, which is actually self-righteousness, and is as filthy rags (Isaiah 64:6).

I knew her good deeds were simply not good enough. If it were so, one could boast about it. In Eph. 2:8-9, it says "For by grace are ye saved through faith, and that not of yourselves, it is the gift of God. Not by works lest any man should boast." So it had to be by **faith**, simply trusting Jesus to wash all our sins away and believing that what He did for us will save us.

Yes, I believed she was "poor in spirit," knowing she was nothing of herself and had to depend on Him to save her. "For their's is the kingdom of Heaven" (Matt. 5:3), so why do we doubt? Faith bringeth forth good works, else faith would be dead. If ye love me, keep my commandents, and it is only him which withstandeth till the end that shall be saved.

Yes, Naomi did believe in the crucifixion. She had saved an article that had been printed in the daily paper one year which described in detail the crucifixion of Christ. It technically explained the physical pain of such a death. Naomi read this article every year on Good Friday. She had a clear vision of Christ suffering on the cross. I believe she also understood **why** Christ died such a death.

After her life of serving others and then suffering an end like she did, I wished her a peaceful life in heaven with all my heart. One day, very suddenly, a new thought struck me. She suffered a martyr's death! Her hands and feet were tied while being tortured. They wanted her to cooperate in things which her conscience would not allow her to do. She must have known it would mean more torturing or death if she did not cooperate. She may have thought they might release her if she cooperated yet, even then, she didn't. Her faith withstood until death. She died like Jesus, our perfect example, not resisting or fighting back.

"But I say unto you, That ye resist not evil: but whosoever shall smite thee on thy right cheek, turn to him the other also" (Matt. 5:39). But she did resist the evil part they wanted her to play. She "resisted unto blood, striving against sin" (Heb. 12:4). She kept His commandments until death.

"Blessed are they which are persecuted for righteousness' sake: for their's is the kingdom of heaven." Do we believe this promise? It made me feel so good to have these thoughts about Naomi's death and I had to share them with someone. I talked to Mother about it and she said she had thought the same thing.

After several years, some of our fears of being alone remain, especially at night, but it's not quite so keen anymore, for which we are so thankful. "Sorrow or tragedy never leaves you as it found you" proves to be very true. We can become bitter or better through it—the choice is ours.

One can read so many nice verses in the Book of Psalms pertaining to how the Lord protects us. Why wasn't Naomi protected? We have finally reached the conclusion that He does not always protect our physical bodies, but He will protect our souls for life everlasting if we ask for His help. Be not afraid of them which kill the body, but are not able to kill the soul: But rather fear him, which after he hath killed, hath power to cast into hell (Luke 12:4-5). I believe Naomi's guardian angel was right there and helped her across the Jordan into those beautiful mansions.

Another spring finally arrived, bringing life and hope again. One day as Rebecca and I were walking home from Tresslers, we walked past the Biller home and saw our new neighbors working in their lawn. We walked up to them and soon they were asking questions concerning Naomi. They said they got the house at a cheap figure, but at first they had some qualms about moving into it. One thing they felt they had to do was to tear all the partitions out of the basement. They also said it disturbs them that traffic slows down sometimes while driving past their house and people staring in. Sometimes people even stop and look in.

Many times we wonder what our thoughts would have been these past several years if this had not happened, for it changed our whole thought pattern. We have finally quit trying to analyze the purpose in it because there are too many unanswered questions. If we keep asking why, we only hear our own echo. It would be so nice to think of Naomi sometimes without thinking of how she died. An ordinary death would seem sweet, but we simply must make the best of it. One cannot buy experience. Part of it can be felt with a handshake, part of it with words, but the greatest part is not to be expressed.

We now place more value on life and we also find our thoughts traveling heavenward a lot more. We find we have more compassion for others in time of need. We need to cling to all these little details to seek a silver lining amidst the dark clouds. Our lives can be enriched by it if we let it. The more often gold is put through fire, the purer it becomes.

Sometime in July 1984 there was another article in the daily paper concerning Anderson, stating how he fired his attorney and will appeal for a new trial. He might have deceived many others at his trial into believing that he is remorseful by his actions and by carrying a Bible, but he hadn't deceived us. Oh, how glad we would be if he would still come to know Christ, be born again, and become a child of God. Christ died to set the vilest sinner free.

One evening in September 1984, I decided I would try to call Henry Johnson who had been the foreman of the jury at Danny's trial in Easton. We had never spoken one word with any of the jurors because we hadn't been present after the deliberations but knew they would have liked to talk with us.

I finally got in contact with Johnson by calling information. When I introduced myself as a Huyard from New Holland, I asked him if the name sounded familiar to make sure I had the right Johnson. He replied, "It sure does." He then asked many questions, saying they wanted so much to talk with us and they often wondered what happened with Anderson. I gave him the details of his trial. He wondered what kind of guy he is and what size he is. I told him he is about Danny's size and described what we saw of his character. After this description, he sort of gasped and said, "We had pictured Anderson as a tall guy and some kind of monster, with Danny following on behind." After I told him of Danny's prior police record, he could hardly believe it. He said that many times, while deliberating, they would have liked to ask us questions, but of course this was entirely against the law.

Also in September 1984, we had Detective Henry and his family and Trooper Nettles at our home for dinner. We spent a nice evening together. They are very nice, respectful people and we will hardly ever forget that visit. We think about them many times. After that last visit, we felt as if another chapter of our lives had closed and it was time to move on to new beginnings.

The wise man Solomon wrote: There is a time and a season for every purpose under the sun: A time to be born and a time to die. A time to plant and a time to pluck that which was planted. A time to weep and a time to laugh...." In Romans 12:15 it tells us to rejoice with them that do rejoice and to weep with them who weep.

When we feel fearful as darkness descends around us, we will remember these verses from the Bible:

"And the peace of God, which passeth all understanding shall keep your hearts and minds through Jesus Christ. Finally, brethren, whatsoever things are true, whatsoever things are honest, whatsoever things are just, whatsoever things are pure, whatsoever things are lovely, whatsoever things are of good report; if there be any virtue, and if there be any praise, think on these things" (Phil. 4:7-8).

—— Epilogue ——

It is now 1992, eight years after this journal was written and ten years after the tragedy. I hope that anyone who reads this will take it at its value, for it is not my wish to offend anyone.

A lot of changes have come about in these years. In 1988, I married a sincere, loving husband who had been a widower with four loving children. We have also been blessed with a baby daughter who joined us in 1990.

Aunt Mary continues to live by herself as she has done since Naomi passed away. Watching her little sister grow up and living with her for fifty years and then suddenly losing her one day created a tremendous loss and loneliness for her.

Soon after this unfortunate event, I asked Mary one day what she had done with the cauliflower that Naomi froze that day. She admitted that she had thrown it away.

Mary also had asked Detective Henry when Naomi's clothing and basket would be returned. He replied that these items would remain sealed until all the appeals were completed. After ten years, she has not yet received them. She would have preferred to have had the coat returned because it was newly-made by herself and had no marks on it in spite of what had happened.

After experiencing such an unusual death in our family, it was hard to express our thoughts and feelings to the company who visited us. Those times when we did express ourselves too freely, it was said that we could not accept the happening. Then at other times when we did not express ourselves, it was said that we bottled things up and could not accept the happening. We could not win, and we gave up trying. It definitely was a learning experience.

Sometimes we have a strong urge to visit the boys in prison, although it is not permitted for the victim's family to do so. This is understandable to some respect, but also unfortunate if you have a desire to help the defendant. How do you help one who has led a hardened life after a rough childhood? And how do you go about helping another one who seems to have been a born loser and has been to the State Correctional Center, Juvenile Center, and Christian social workers, but has ended up participating in a murder?

Danny Biller (whose name was changed in this book) is in a prison in Pittsburgh, Pennsylvania, and Anderson (name was also changed) is at Camp Hill, Pennsylvania. The only other names changed in this book were Danny Biller's parents and the foreman of the jury at Danny's trial.

We spoke with a reporter who has visited both of them. She said that Danny continues to be labeled with problems, and that Anderson denies that he was ever involved in the murder and says that he never saw the Amish woman and is innocently convicted. He has brainwashed himself into actually believing this.

Anderson showed his tatoos of knives on both his arms and a skeleton with a knife pierced through it on his chest. He then boasted that the reporter hadn't seen the best yet and lifted his T-shirt to reveal his back with a snake wrapped around an upside-down cross. He persistently said that he is not a Satan-worshipper, but that the investigators tried to make him appear as if he was by deliberately numbering his court proceedings with the number "666."

Ironically, his court manuscripts were numbered "666," although it was not done deliberately. One has to wonder if Anderson knows what the number "666" represents. And, why does it bother him?

Since this number represents the beast or Satan, it is a comforting thought to know that Naomi did not bow to the beast—instead, she resisted unto the blood and did not give into the sinful desires of Biller and Anderson.

Therefore, the Lord blessed her and also protected her body from being defiled in spite of the boys' efforts. What would be a better way to enter into eternity than with a pure body and spirit? Her death has a triumphant ring to it.

What a contrast to the two wasted lives in prison here on earth, and also thousands of others like them. Everyone of them had once been a mother's innocent baby....

No, Naomi's death is not sad compared to these wasted lives.

What is a solution to this? What are **we** doing to help these prisoners realize the true importance of life as well as life after death? What are **we** doing to tell them about Christ and His love and the New Birth? If we don't go to the prison ourselves and tell them the Good News, it is our responsibility to always pray for them, the chaplains, and evangelists who visit the prisons.

It is our wish that the hearts of Biller and Anderson would be touched and that their souls be saved before the day of judgement. All suffering would be a blessing if this would happen. We would like to ask all Christians to pray for them. The Holy Spirit can yet perform miracles! Satan can be overruled! Let's not underestimate the power of prayer. We wish them the love of God in their hearts and a peace which passeth all understanding.

The book of Job is an inspiration for all who suffer tragedies. Why did Job need to suffer so much, and who was the instigator? The Bible tells us that it was Satan, and the Lord allowed it. Through Job's steadfast faithfulness in Christ, he was overwhelmingly blessed at a later date. Let us all believe this simply-told story and follow Job's example.